Compliments of
(Phil Kassens)
Divine Diet Ministries, Inc.
102 N. Fairground St
Liberty, Indiana 47353
(317) 458-6795

Tragedy in the Church:

The Missing Gifts

Also available as
The Tozer Pulpit, Volume 7

Tragedy in the Church:

The Missing Gifts

Twelve sermons relating
to the life and ministry
of the Christian Church

Edited and Compiled
by Gerald B. Smith

christian publications, inc.

25 South Tenth Street, Harrisburg, PA 17101

The Mark of *CP* Vibrant Faith

Printed in the United States of America

ISBN 0-87509-215-2

Contents

Preface

Dr. A. W. Tozer, during his fruitful preaching ministry, was concerned about the spiritual shortcomings of the visible Christian churches.

His preaching from week to week always displayed love and appreciation and concern for the church, the true Body of Christ on earth. The pattern of his preaching revealed a consistent yearning that every assembly of Christian believers would realize its full potential in producing spiritual fruit for the honor of Jesus Christ.

Fifteen years after the passing of Dr. Tozer, Christian Publications, Inc., is pleased to release this seventh volume in the Tozer Pulpit Series, the first to deal exclusively with subjects related to the Christian church and the spiritual basis for its varied and continuing ministries.

As we have done in the past, we point out that Dr. Tozer's sermons are not to be read as textbooks in a doctrinal sense. His appeal chapter by chapter is more likely to be devotional and inspirational.

We are truly thankful for the continuing demand for Dr. Tozer's edited sermons, the only available source for his often-prophetic and incisive material since his death in May 1963.

The Publisher

Chapter One

God's Eternal Work:
Only by the Holy Spirit

*And gave gifts unto men . . . he gave some, apostles;
and some, prophets; and some, evangelists; and some,
pastors and teachers; for the perfecting of the saints,
for the work of the ministry, for the edifying of the
body of Christ. Ephesians 4:8, 11-12*

The scriptural teaching that the work of God
through the church can be accomplished only by the
energizing of the Holy Spirit is very hard for humans
to accept, for it is a concept that frustrates our own
carnal desire for honor and praise, for glory and recognition.

Basically, God has been very kind and tender with
us—but there is no way in which He can compromise
with our human pride and carnality. That is why His
Word bears down so hard on "proud flesh," insisting

9

that we understand and confess that no human gifts, no human talents can accomplish the ultimate and eternal work of God.

Even though God has faithfully reminded us that it is a ministry of the Holy Spirit to submerge and hide the Christian worker in the work, the true humility He seeks among us is still too often the exception and not the rule.

I think we ought to be mature enough to confess that many have been converted to Christ and have come into the church without wrestling with that human desire for honor and praise. As a result, some have actually spent a lifetime in religious work doing little more than getting glory for themselves!

Brethren, the glory can belong only to God! If we take the glory, God is being frustrated in the church.

With this background, let us consider the Apostle's account of what Jesus Christ actually did:

He gave special gifts "for the perfecting of the saints for the work of the ministry for the edifying of the body of Christ" (Eph. 4:12).

Did you notice that we have purposely eliminated the commas? God did not put the commas in this passage—the translators did!

The commas make the passage read as though there are three separate results of these gifts in the Body of Christ.

The work of the ministry which the saints are to do will bring about the edifying of the Body of Christ—and this is not just in reference to the ordained ministry as we know it. It is the ministry of all Christians to have some share in the building up of the Body of Christ until we all come into the unity of the faith and of the knowledge of the Son of God unto a perfect man, with a measure of the stature of the fullness of Christ.

It is rather common for visitors in our church to ask me frankly about some of the things they do not find in our fellowship. They want to know why we frown on some customs found in other contemporary groups.

I try very hard to keep from drawing uncomplimentary comparisons with other churches and other groups. If there are failures in meeting high spiritual and scriptural standards, God will have to deal with us, no matter who we are.

But we are responsible to our Lord for the conduct of the work which He has given us and we have prayerfully studied the Scriptures to determine how we can fit into those methods through which God accomplishes His eternal work.

I think that there are three basic methods whereby God uses the Body of Christ to do His final work—His eternal work.

First, Christian believers and Christian congregations must be thoroughly consecrated to Christ's glory alone. This means absolutely turning our backs on the modern insistence for human glory and recognition.

I have done everything I can to keep "performers" out of my pulpit. We do not think we are called to recognize "performers." We are confident that our Lord never meant for the Christian church to provide a kind of religious stage where performers proudly take their bows, seeking human recognition for themselves.

We do not believe that is God's way to an eternal work. He has never indicated that proclamation of the gospel is to become dependent upon human performances.

Instead, it is important to note how much the Bible

11

has to say about the common people, the plain people —like you and me.

The Word of God speaks with such appreciation of the common people that I am inclined to believe it is a term dear to God.

Jesus was always surrounded by the common people. He had a few "stars," but largely His helpers were from the common people, the good people—and surely, not always the most brilliant.

Jesus looked first for consecration and in our own day it is surely true that His Spirit uses those who are no longer interested in their own promotion, but are consecrated to one thought—getting glory for Jesus Christ, who is Saviour and Lord!

To please God, a person must be just an instrument for God to use.

For a few seconds, picture in your mind the variety of wonderful and useful appliances we have in our homes. They have been engineered and built to perform tasks of all kinds.

But without the inflow of electrical power they are just lumps of metal and plastic, unable to function and serve. They cannot do their work until power is applied from a dynamic outside source.

So it is in the work of God in the church.

Many persons preach and teach. Many take part in the music. Certain ones try to administer God's work— but if the power of God's Spirit does not have freedom to energize all they do, these workers might just as well have stayed home.

Natural gifts are not enough in God's work. The mighty Spirit of God must have freedom to animate and quicken with His overtones of creativity and blessing.

There have been great preachers in the past who were in demand all over the world. I think of one of the greatest, a recognized divine in New England. We still may think of him as an evangelical, but he was not known primarily as a Bible preacher. He expounded on such subjects as nature and science, literature and philosophy. His books had instant sales and his pulpit oratory attracted great crowds.

But when that preacher died, the bottom just dropped out of all the work which had kept him so busy. The work of the Spirit of God had been given no place in directing all of that natural talent and energy. God's eternal work had not been furthered.

We may recall, however, that when Spurgeon and G. Campbell Morgan passed away, their work and outreach went right on. Both of these well-known preachers had built their lifetime ministries on the Word of God and the power of the Spirit.

You can write it down as a fact: no matter what a man does, no matter how successful he seems to be in any field, if the Holy Spirit is not the chief energizer of his activity, it will all fall apart when he dies.

Perhaps the saddest part about that is that the man may be honored at his death for his talents and abilities, but he will learn the truth in that great day when our Lord judges the work of every man. That which is solely his own work and is wrought by his own talent will be recognized as nothing but wood, hay and stubble.

A second important element in God's use of the believing church is His response to our prayers raised to Him in true faith.

This matter of prayer really bears in on the great privileges of the common people, the children of God.

13

No matter what our stature or status, we have the authority in the family of God to pray the prayer of faith, that prayer that can engage the heart of God and that can meet God's conditions of spiritual life and victory.

Our consideration of the power and efficacy of prayer enters into the question of why we are a Christian congregation and what we are striving to be and do.

We have to consider whether we are just going around and around—like a religious merry-go-round. Are we just holding on to the painted mane of the painted horse, repeating a trip of very insignificant circles to a pleasing musical accompaniment?

Some may think the path of the religious carousel is a kind of progress, but the family of God knows better than that. We are among those who believe in something more than holding religious services in the same old weekly groove. We believe that in an assembly of redeemed believers there should be marvelous answers to prayer.

We believe that God hears and actually answers our praying in the Spirit. Let it be said that one miraculous answer to prayer within a congregation will do more to lift and encourage and solidify the people of God than almost any other thing.

Answers to our prayers will lift up the hands that hang down in discouragement and strengthen the feeble spiritual knees.

I do believe that all of the advertising we can do in a variety of ways will never equal the interest and participation in the things of God resulting from the gracious answers to the prayers of faith generated by the Holy Spirit.

Actually, it will be such prayer and the meeting of God's conditions which will turn loose the third method

14

of God's ordained accomplishments through the church. I speak of the Christian's dependence on the Holy Spirit and the willingness to exercise the Spirit's gifts.

This is an overflowing subject, one not easily exhausted, leading us into consideration of the presence and power and blessings of God available only through the ministries of His Spirit.

There are very few perceptive Christians who will argue with the fact that the gentle presence of the divine Spirit is always necessary if we are to see revival wonders.

I still have in my files an old sermon outline on revival in the church. I preached on revival when I was young; I soon found out it was easy to preach revival sermons but very difficult to make them come to life in the churches.

What do I mean by "revival wonders"?

Well, you will find such wonders among the people of God when someone in the congregation steps out into a new and wonderful spiritual experience. Just let that happen to one young person and it will do more to cause the youth work to lift and move and get off the sandbar than a host of scheduled meetings and special conferences.

The same is certainly true of older Christians. Just let one person step out in faith, claiming the fullness of the Spirit, crowning Jesus Christ as Lord, and the spiritual fallout will be felt and enjoyed by the entire group of believers.

I think we have to accept this and believe it as a spiritual principle, according to God's promises concerning the Holy Spirit.

We do not believe such spiritual blessings can be bought.

We do not believe that a true spirit and work of

15

revival can be brought in by airplane or by freight. We do not believe that God's presence and blessings in the souls of men can be humanly induced.

We believe such revival wonders can take place only as the Holy Spirit energizes the Word of God as it is preached. Genuine blessings cannot come unless the Holy Spirit energizes and convinces and stirs the people of God.

Now, what does this all add up to? If we are intent upon God's glory alone, if we are using the resources of prayer and if we are obedient to the Spirit of God, there will assuredly be an attitude of true joyfulness in Christ's church.

Now, you who know me probably do not think of me as an overwhelmingly cheerful man. But, thank God, I know about the true joy of the Lord and I believe we should be a joyful people.

Each member of the Body of Christ must face up to the question of whether or not we actually fit the description of "a joyful people."

How many of you bring family and domestic problems right along with you, in thought and mind, when you come to worship?

How many businessmen bring their weekday troubles home on Friday night and carry them along to church on Sunday?

When income tax time rolls around, how many of you react by getting down in the dumps?

And what about the family's health? the worries about the children? How many of God's people continue to lug these worries and problems around on a fulltime basis?

We ought not to do it and we cannot be a joyful people if we do!

Why should the children of the King go mourning all the day? Why should the children of the King hang their heads and tote their own burdens?

Brethren, we are missing the mark about Christian victory and the life of joy in our Saviour. We ought to be standing straight and praising our God!

I must agree with the psalmist that the joy of the Lord is still the strength of His people. I do believe that the sad world is attracted to spiritual sunshine—the genuine thing, that is.

Some churches train their greeters and ushers to smile, showing as many teeth as possible. But I can sense that kind of display—and when I am greeted by a man who is smiling because he has been trained to smile, I know I am shaking the flipper of a trained seal.

But when the warmth and delight and joy of the Holy Spirit are in a congregation and the folks are just spontaneously joyful and unable to hide their happy grin, the result is a wonderful influence and effect upon others.

I am sure I have said a hundred times that the reason we have to search for so many things to cheer us up is the fact that we are not really joyful and contentedly happy within.

I admit that we live in a gloomy world and that international affairs, nuclear rumors and threats, earthquakes and riots cause people to shake their heads in despair and say, "What's the use?"

But we are Christians, and Christians have every right to be the happiest people in the world. We do not have to look to other sources—for we look to the Word of God and discover how we can know the faithful God above and draw from His resources!

Another promise of God is that the Holy Spirit with His gifts and graces will also give us genuine love for one another.

I will tell you this: I am determined that I am going to love everybody, even if it kills me! I have set my heart on it. I am going to do it.

Some people are just naturally winsome and love-able—but then there are others of whom some have said that only their mothers could love them. But I am determined that I am going to love them for Christ's sake!

Some people don't like me—and they have said so. But I am going to love them and they are not going to be able to stop me.

Brethren, love is not just feeling—love is willing. You can will to love people. The Lord says to me, "Love people!" I know very well that He does not mean just to feel love for them. He means that I should will to love them!

I think it would be wrong to mention the blessed things the Holy Spirit wants to do in our midst and not add sympathy and compassion to the list.

I dare to trust that we are a sympathetic body of believers. I hope that none of us can ever hear of a fellow Christian being in trouble or experiencing trials without feeling concern, suffering over it and taking the matter to God in prayer.

This kind of concern for one another comes out of love and understanding. If we have this grace by God's Spirit, we will take no superior attitudes; we will not be censorious of others.

Every one of us should be keenly aware of the fact that if the Lord should take His hand from under us, we would all plunge down and be gone forever. We thank God for His goodness, which He continues to reveal to us in spite of our many weaknesses and faults.

It is in this context that I recall a conversation with a devoted English brother, Noel Palmer, a tall, expressive Salvation Army fellow with a great voice.

I said to him, "Brother Palmer, what about sanctification in the heart? What does it mean to you?"

He quickly responded.

"I believe that if the heart loves God and wants to do right, God will overlook a lot of flaws—and He will give us light as we walk with Him!"

I say with him, thank God you don't have to be flawless to be blessed!

You need to have a big heart that desires and wants the will of God more than anything else in the world. You need also to have an eye single to His glory.

These are the things that matter—exercising the gifts of God's Spirit by the energy of the Spirit.

These are the things that must be important to us in our congregational fellowship, all adding up to the fact that the Holy Spirit is making Jesus Christ our chief joy and delight!

Chapter Two

Gifts of the Spirit:
Necessity in the Church

So we, being many, are one body in Christ, and every one members one of another. Having then gifts differing according to the grace that is given to us . . . Romans 12:5-6

Now there are diversities of gifts, but the same Spirit. And there are differences of administrations, but the same Lord. And there are diversities of operations, but it is the same God which worketh all in all. But the manifestation of the Spirit is given to every man to profit withal. 1 Corinthians 12:4-7

The Bible teaches us that the genuine gifts of the Holy Spirit are a necessity in the spiritual life and ministries of every Christian congregation serious about glorifying Jesus Christ as Saviour and Lord.

Having said that, I also must add that I do not

know of any group or denomination or communion anywhere in the world that has come into full and per-fect realization of the Pauline doctrine and goal of spiritual life in the believing Body of Christ.

Now that is a conclusion that may not give much encouragement to the critical and restless ones who seem to be found in nearly every Christian fellowship—apparently just perched and ready to fly away to more spiritual pastures as soon as they can locate a perfect congregation made up of perfect people and led by a perfect minister!

It seems to me that Paul was trying to make it as plain as he could in his epistles that any segment of the Body of Christ, anywhere in the world, should re-capitulate—gather up and sum up within itself—all of the offices and gifts and workings of the entire church of Christ.

A careful study of the Apostle's teachings concern-ing Jesus Christ and His church should persuade us that any local assembly ought to demonstrate all of the functions of the whole body. Paul clearly teaches that each Christian believer ought to demonstrate a proper gift or gifts, bestowed by God the Holy Spirit, and that together the believers would accomplish the work of God as a team.

Let us review something here that all of us prob-ably know—the doctrine of the life and operation of Christian believers on earth—starting with the fact that the Christian church is the Body of Christ, with Christ Himself the head of the body.

Every true Christian, no matter where he lives, is a part of that body, and the Holy Spirit is to the church what our own soul is to our physical body. Through the operation of the Holy Spirit, Christ becomes the life, the unity and the consciousness of the body which is the church. Let the soul leave the physical body and all the parts of the body cease to function.

Every human body is thus an apt illustration of the spiritual life and functions of the church. Paul uses the illustration in three of his epistles in the New Testament, indicating really that it is more than an illustration for it is something carefully planned—members designed and created for distinct functions under the control of the head, Jesus Christ.

Illustrations are never perfect and parallels will generally break down at some point, particularly when we come to the sacred and infinite things of God.

For instance, for a man's physical body to function, the members have to be in one place. If you separate the man and scatter him around, he is dead.

But the Body of Christ, the church, does not have to be in one place because it has a unity, the unity of the Spirit. All of the members do not have to be in one place, for many of them are already in heaven, and those on earth are scattered in widely diverse areas.

And yet the true church, the Body of Christ, is not torn nor divided, for it is held together by the Holy Spirit, who maintains the life of the body and controls the functions of the members.

In the illustration of the physical body, the members are all designed for specific functions. The eye is designed for seeing. The ear is designed for hearing. The hand is designed in a most special way to perform distinct functions. The lungs are designed for breathing, the heart for the circulation of the blood.

These are all designed to cooperate and act and serve in concert with each other.

So it is to be in the Body of Christ—and we are

members. According to Paul, the whole body exists for its members and the members exist for the whole body. And that of course is the reason God gives gifts, that the body may profit spiritually and maintain spiritual health and prosperity in its service for Jesus Christ in an unfriendly world.

Now, what about the control of the members? This is the point that many people seem to forget: that all of the effective and cooperating members of the body take their direction from the head.

When a man's head is separated from the rest of his body there can be no more control or direction of those members which had functioned together so well during his lifetime. This is plain physiology—that the physical body must get its control and direction from the head.

It is just as plain in Bible teaching that the church, the Body of Christ, must get its life and control and direction from its living head, Jesus Christ our Lord!

Every Christian, then, should be vitally concerned and personally interested in what the Bible tells us about the functions of the members.

These functions—called gifts in the Bible—are special abilities; they are gifts from God out of the store of His grace.

Paul wrote to the Roman church this reminder: "For I say, through the grace given unto me, to every man that is among you, not to think of himself more highly than he ought to think; but to think soberly, according as God hath dealt to every man the measure of faith" (12:3).

Paul then makes it plain that all believers in the church had been given "gifts differing according to the grace that is given to us" (v. 6).

Some teachers seem to think that they know exactly how many gifts of the Spirit are mentioned in the New Testament letters, but I say it is difficult to be dogmatic about the total number. It is certainly possible that some of the designations are synonomous with one another, such as gifts of ruling and gifts of government, and no doubt there is some overlapping in the varied gift functions.

In the twelfth chapter of First Corinthians, where Paul writes about the diversities of gifts, nine are mentioned specifically. Later in the same chapter he speaks of God setting apostles, prophets and teachers in the church and mentions such other gifts as helps and governments.

In the twelfth chapter of Romans, Paul makes reference to the gifts of exhortation, of giving, of ruling and of showing mercy.

In chapter four of Ephesians, mention is made of the gift functions of evangelists and pastors.

Concerning the apostles, it is generally agreed among Christians everywhere that the apostles chosen by Jesus had a particular office which has not been perpetuated. They were personal witnesses of the life and ministry of Christ Himself.

The New Testament gift of prophecy was not to predict—but to tell forth what God has to say and to proclaim God's truth for the present age.

We cannot deny that Christian teachers should have a special gift. Let us not be afraid to admit that not everyone can teach. Even those with natural capabilities must have a special anointing from the Spirit of God to impart truth. This is undoubtedly true also of the special gifts of wisdom and knowledge.

The basic spiritual life within the Body of Christ

has always humbly acknowledged the sovereignty of the Spirit of God in gifts of miracles and healing. Paul concludes his references to the gifts in writing to the Corinthians by reference to diversities of tongues, and then asks the rhetorical question:

"Are all apostles? are all prophets? are all teachers? are all workers of miracles? Have all the gifts of healing? do all speak with tongues? do all interpret?" (1 Cor. 12:29-30).

The answer to these questions, of course, is no, for Paul then instructs:

"But covet earnestly the best gifts: and yet shew I unto you a more excellent way" (v. 31).

It has been suggested to me that all Christian groups that believe in the authenticity and necessity of the gifts of the Spirit in the church in our time should be able to stand together in a great unity of fellowship.

I can only say here what I have often said to many of my friends in the groups associated with what is called "the tongues movement." I do not believe it is proper to magnify one gift above all others, particularly when that gift is one that Paul described as of least value.

I cannot believe that the unscriptural exhibition of that gift in public, like a child with a new toy, can be pleasing to God.

I believe that in any setting, the tendency to place personal feeling above the Scriptures is always an insult to God.

Where the wise and gentle Spirit of God is in control, believers ought to exhibit genuine discernment. In some "gifted" circles today, there is an almost total lack of spiritual discernment and a credulity beyond belief, revealed in many splits and divisions, acceptance of immature child preachers, and the use of a kind of gospel "rock and roll" music long before Elvis Presley.

With this review I am certainly not condemning individuals or churches or groups on a blanket basis. But there are some who say, "We have the gifts of the Spirit—come and join us!"

Before I join a movement, a school of thought, a theological persuasion, or a church group or denomination, I must make the proper tests.

What have been the characteristics and the earmarks of that group over a long period of years? Is there an exercise of sharp spiritual discernment that knows the flesh from the spirit? Is there an emphasis on spiritual cohesion and unity? Is there a scriptural emphasis on purity of life or is there a careless attitude concerning moral living?

For our fundamentalist Christian circles in general, I fear that there is an alarming lack of spiritual discernment. Because we have shut out the Holy Spirit in so many ways, we are stumbling along as though we are spiritually blindfolded. Ruling out the discernment and leadership of the Holy Spirit is the only possible explanation for the manner in which Christian churches have yielded to the temptation to entertain, entertain!

There is no other explanation for the wave of rationalism that now marks the life of many congregations. And what about the increasing compromise with all of the deadening forces of worldliness? The true, humble and uncompromising church of Christ is harder and harder to find.

It is not because leaders and men and women in the church are bad—it is only because the Holy Spirit of God has been so forcefully shut out and the needful gift of discernment about spiritual things is no longer present.

I believe we definitely need the gift of faith, and I do not mean that faith that we all must exercise to be saved. I believe we need men and women with a special and peculiar gift of faith, which often links with the gift of discernment by the Spirit.

There is a simple gift function of helps. I do not know all that it means, but I know many Christians who are just to be helpers in the work of Christ.

Related to that is the gift of showing mercy; going about doing good and encouraging the discouraged, as Jesus did so often.

There is a gift of government in the church, and it may be the same as the gift of ruling.

Some may not know that there is a true gift of giving. All believers are taught to give—but there is such a thing as a special gift of giving.

The Bible also speaks of the gift function of the evangelist and the pastor in the church.

God has given us in His Holy Spirit every gift and power and help that we need to serve Him. We do not have to look around for some other way.

The most solemn aspect of this is our individual responsibility. The Bible teaches that a day is coming when we must all appear before the judgment seat of Christ; that everyone faces a review of the things done in his body, whether good or bad.

In that day we will be fully exposed and the things that we have done in our own strength and for our own glory will be quickly blown away like worthless straw and stubble, forever separated from the kind of deeds and ministries which were wrought by the Spirit and which are described as eternal treasures in the sight of God, gold and silver and precious stones that the fire cannot harm.

In that day, all that is related to the work of the flesh will perish and pass away, and only that which has been wrought by the Spirit of God will remain and stand.

Do you dare to accept the fact that the sovereign God had designed to do all of His work through spiritually-gifted men and women? Therefore, He does all of His work on earth through humble and faithful believers who are given spiritual gifts and abilities beyond their own capacities.

Let me shock you at this point: A naturally bright person can carry on religious activity without a special gift from God. Filling church pulpits every week are some who are using only natural abilities and special training. Some are known as Bible expositors, for it is possible to read and study commentaries and then repeat what has been learned about the Scriptures.

Yes, it may shock you, but it is true that anyone able to talk fluently can learn to use religious phrases and can become recognized as a preacher.

But if any man is determined to preach so that his work and ministry will abide in the day of the judgment fire, then he must preach, teach and exhort with the kind of love and concern that comes only through a true and genuine gift of the Holy Spirit—something beyond his own capabilities!

We need to remember that even our Lord Jesus Christ ministering in the time of His humanity among us, depended upon the anointing of the Spirit. He applied the words of the prophet to Himself when He said, "The Spirit of the Lord is upon me, because he hath anointed me to preach the gospel to the poor; . . .

and recovering of sight to the blind, to set at liberty them that are bruised" (Luke 4:18).

Do we realize that when leaders and members of a church do not have the genuine gifts of the Spirit—the true anointing of the Spirit—they are thrown back to depend upon human and natural capabilities?

In that case, natural talents must come to the fore.

We hear that some fellow can whistle through his teeth. Someone else has marvelous talent for impromptu composition of poetry. Some musicians are talented composers and singers. Others are talented talkers— let's admit it!

So in this realm of religious activity, talent runs the church. The gifts of the Spirit are not recognized and used as God intended.

Also, much of church activity and fellowship falls back upon the practice of psychology. Many leaders in church groups are skilled and masterful psychologists. They know how to handle people and get the crowds to come, and the operation qualifies as an amazingly "successful" church.

Part of the successful operation of that church depends upon men with business talents and part of it depends upon men with natural gifts as salesmen and politicians.

I say that a Christian congregation can survive and often appear to prosper in the community by the exercise of human talent and without any touch from the Holy Spirit! All that religious activity and the dear people will not know anything better until the great and terrible day when our self-employed talents are burned with fire and only that which was wrought by the Holy Ghost will stand forever!

Through His Spirit, God is waiting and willing to

do for us or for any church what He waits to do for the entire Body of Christ!

It was the promise of Christ that "you shall receive power" through the ministry of the Holy Spirit, and the disciples were taught that the Holy Spirit would also bestow sweet graces and pleasant fruits of godliness when He could gain control of our persons.

Let me share my earnest hope and expectation with you—I believe the Holy Spirit of God wants to do some gracious new thing in our midst!

With the dignity and self-control that is basic to the Christian faith, the calmness and sweetness that belonged to Jesus Christ, and the abandonment that marked the spiritual life of the apostles in the early church, let us throw ourselves out on the great fullness of God with expectation!

Wouldn't it be a wonderful thing if that outpouring of the Spirit of God which came to the Moravians centuries ago would come upon us again? They could only explain, "It was a sense of the loving nearness of the Saviour instantaneously bestowed."

Oh, what that would do for us—a sense of the loving nearness of the Saviour instantaneously bestowed! With it comes a love for God's Word, loving cohesion, dignity, usefulness, high moral living and purity of life —because that's the only kind of nearness the Holy Spirit ever brings!

Chapter Three

Tragedy in the Church: The Missing Gifts

But the manifestation of the Spirit is given to every man to profit withal. 1 Corinthians 12:7

The Christian church cannot rise to its true stature in accomplishing the purposes of God when its members operate largely through the gifts of nature, neglecting the true gifts and graces of the Spirit of God.

Much of the religious activity we see in the churches is not the eternal working of the Eternal Spirit, but the mortal working of man's mortal mind—and that is raw tragedy!

From what I see and sense in evangelical circles, I would have to say that about ninety per cent of the religious work carried on in the churches is being done by ungifted members.

I am speaking in this context of men and women

who know how to do many things but fail to display the spiritual gifts promised through the Holy Spirit.

This is one of the very evident ways in which we have slowed down the true working of God in His church and in the hearts of unbelieving men all around us—acknowledging and allowing ungifted members of the body to do religious work without possessing the genuine gifts of the Spirit.

I expect I will hear a reply to this assessment. Someone will say, "Well, that's just Tozer's private view!"

But in recent conferences, such as the International Fellowship of Evangelical Students, the counter-part of Inter-Varsity in Canada, it has been gratifying to fellowship with internationally-known ministers who are preaching about the great need for the Spirit's operation among the people of God. This conviction is being echoed and re-echoed throughout the world as our Lord is confirming the same need to many thousands in denominations everywhere.

Now, someone else will ask, "Why this emphasis? Doesn't every Christian have the Holy Spirit?"

Yes—there is plenty of Biblical authority that every regenerated believer does have a measure of the Spirit!

Paul wrote to the Corinthian church and reminded the believers that they were all baptized into one body by the Spirit. Paul also wrote to the church at Rome insisting that "if any man have not the Spirit of Christ, he is none of his" (8:9).

But in the same letter in which he explained to the Corinthian Christians the operation of the Spirit of God in their regeneration, he also told them: "I do not want you to be ignorant about spiritual gifts," and then, "Covet earnestly the best gifts."

I think it is plain that if Paul only wanted them to know that they have a measure of the Spirit upon conversion, he would have said that and stopped right there.

But he went on at great length to explain the necessity for the functioning of the gifts of the Spirit in the church—and I believe he was explaining that these spiritual functions and capabilities are the birthright of every Christian.

Paul did not say we must be important and well-known Christians to be useful to the Spirit of God in the functioning of Christ's Body, the church. This is not something reserved for the great. It is the birthright of the most humble saint.

Paul reminded the Corinthian Christians that God was actually seeking the simple people because they were willing to respond to the outworking of God's plan through the Holy Spirit and His functions.

"Where is the wise?" Paul asked them. "Where is the scribe? where is the disputer of this world? . . .

"But God hath chosen the foolish things of the world to confound the wise; and God hath chosen the weak things of the world to confound the things which are mighty" (1 Cor. 1:20, 27).

So, brethren, the Spirit of God, His presence and His gifts are not only desirable in our Christian congregations, but absolutely imperative!

Now here is another aspect of truth often overlooked:

The regenerated, converted men and women who joyfully have found their place in the Body of Christ by faith are still humans—even though redeemed through faith in the death and resurrection of Jesus Christ. Having found divine forgiveness through God's mercy and grace, they delight in the complete lifting of the sense of guilt and in the fellowship they find in varied segments of the visible church of Jesus Christ here on earth—here and now.

My point is this—they still are human and they are living in bodies as yet unredeemed! If they are to continue in the blessing of the fellowship of the spiritually redeemed, if they are to successfully engage in the Christian witness God expects of them, they must consciously know and experience the indwelling illumination of the Holy Spirit of God. They must depend upon His gifts and His enduement and His anointing if they hope to cope with the universal blight which is upon mankind.

Believers are yet in their unredeemed bodies. This is true of every believer, every member of the Body—whether the oldest and sweetest saint of God that has followed on to know the Lord or the newest convert that has just found forgiveness of sins and the joy of salvation!

Yes, brethren, this is orthodox Christian theology, and this is how the apostle Paul revealed it to us:

"For the creature was made subject to vanity; not willingly, but by reason of him who hath subjected the same in hope, because the creature itself also shall be delivered from the bondage of corruption into the glorious liberty of the children of God. For we know that the whole creation groaneth and travaileth in pain together until now.

"And not only they, but ourselves also, which have the firstfruits of the Spirit, even we ourselves groan within ourselves, waiting for the adoption, to wit, the redemption of our body" (Rom. 8:20-23).

There is no other way we can have it—the saints of God in this age do live in an unredeemed temple. The body is potentially redeemed for that is the promise of God. But in this life it is not yet actually redeemed.

That is why we take the theme for this message—it is impossible for God to use men and women who yet must die to bring about His eternal purpose. The Eternal Spirit alone can do that kind of an eternal work.

Perhaps we need an illustration here.

The accomplished artist gives his hands and eyes credit for his paintings.

The musician gives his hands and fingers credit for the harmonies produced from keys and the strings of instruments.

Talented people everywhere think that their feet or their hands, their ears or their vocal chords are the means of their productions.

There never was a greater mistake than to believe that!

The credit all has to go to the marvelous brain that God has given every man. The hands have never really done anything except at the bidding and control of the brain.

If the brain should suddenly be cut off and die, the hands will lie limp and helpless. It is the brain of a man that paints a picture, smells a rose, hears the sound of music.

This is all a matter of common physiology. All of us learned this fact in school and doctors know it well in an advanced way. Your hand does not originate anything. If you crochet or paint, cut or trim, operate a machine—the origination and control rests with the brain and the hands function only as the instrument and organ through which the brain works.

The Holy Spirit must be to the members of the Body of Christ what the brain is to eyes and ears and mouth and hands and fingers and feet and toes. The Bible does say "it is God which worketh in you to will and to do . . ." (Phil. 2:13).

Someone may give me credit for something they think I have done for God—but in actuality, God is doing it and using me as an instrument, for there is a sense in which we are unable to do any spiritual work of any kind.

The important thing is that the Holy Spirit desires to take men and women and control them and use them as instruments and organs through which He can express Himself in the Body of Christ.

Perhaps I can use my hands as a further illustration of this truth.

My hands are about average, I suppose. Perhaps a little large for the size of my body. Probably because I had to do a lot of farm work when I was a boy.

But there is something I must tell you about these hands. I cannot play a violin. I have ungifted hands. I cannot paint a picture. I have ungifted hands.

I cannot play the organ or the piano. I can barely hold a screwdriver to do a small repair job to keep things from falling apart at home.

I am perfectly willing to paint a picture, but my hands are ungifted. My brain can give some direction to the members of my body, but there is no response from my brain in the matter of color and form and outline and perspective.

If my brain should say, "Tozer, play something for us on the organ," I could only respond, "Brain, I would love to do it, but my hands know nothing of that gift!"

You will agree that it would be foolish for me to try to bring forth any delightful and satisfying music using such ungifted members as my own hands.

Is it not appalling, then, to think that we allow this very thing to happen in the Body of Christ? We enlist people and tell them to get busy doing God's work—failing to realize the necessity for the Spirit's anointing and control and functioning if a spiritual result is to be produced.

Work that is only religious work and religious activity can be done by ungifted men and women and it can be done within the framework of the Christian church. But it will wind up with the judgment upon it that it is only a product of a human mind.

Let's bring it down to our level.

Religious "activists" have many things of which they can boast. They build churches. They write hymns and books. Musically, they sing and play. Some of them will take time to engage in prayer. Others will organize movements and crusades and campaigns.

No matter how early in the morning they begin and no matter how late at night they stay with their project, if it is an exercise in human talent for religious purposes, it can only wind up as a mortal brain doing a mortal job.

And across it God will write a superscription: "It came to die and it came to go!"

I have taken the pains to say all of this as a reminder that mortality and temporality are written all across the church of Christ in the world today because so many persons are trying to do with human genius and power of the flesh what only God can do through the Holy Spirit.

None of us ought to be fooled by the loose and careless use of the word *immortal*. Art galleries claim that the paintings of Michaelangelo are immortal. In truth, there are no immortal paintings, no immortal sonnets, no immortal musical compositions, for immortality is unending existence.

For myself, I would rather be among those who are unknown, unsung and unheralded doing something through the Spirit of God that will count even a tiny little bit in the kingdom of God, than to be involved in some highly-recognized expression of religious activity across which God will ultimately write the judgment: "This too shall pass!"

It is true that much church work and activity is thrown back upon a shaky foundation of psychology and natural talents.

It is sad but true that many a mother-in-law is actually praying that her handsome son-in-law may be called to preach because he would have such a marvelous "pulpit presence."

We live in a day when charm is supposed to cover almost the entire multitude of sins. Charm has taken a great place in religious expression. Brethren, I am convinced that our Lord expects us to be tough enough and cynical enough to recognize all of this that pleases the unthinking in our churches—the charm stuff, the stage presence in the pulpit, the golden qualities of voice.

We had better not forget what the apostle Paul said about "presence" and "speech."

We accept the fact that Paul was one of the greatest men that ever lived and that he became available as a human channel for a great work by God Almighty.

Do you know what they said about him in his day? The cosmopolitan Corinthians commented that "his letters . . . are weighty and powerful; but his bodily presence is weak, and his speech contemptible" (2 Cor. 10:10).

When they had read his first epistle, they said, "He writes tremendous letters. This is hot stuff!"

But later when they heard him in person, they were disappointed that he seemed to have so few natural talents!

Let us not miss the significance of that assessment. Here is one of the world's greatest minds—but apparently he would have flunked out in any test given radio announcers. He had no charming pulpit presence. He had no golden qualities of voice or manner. But wherever he went he was led by the Holy Spirit. Whatever he did was at the prompting of the Holy Spirit. His great missionary work brought no glory to himself but advanced the cause of Christ throughout the known world of his day.

I feel sorry for the church that decides to call a man to the pulpit because "his personality simply sparkles!"

I have watched quite a few of these sparklers through the years. In reality, as every kid knows at Fourth of July time, sparklers can be an excitement in the neighborhood, but only for about one minute! Then you are left holding a hot stick in your hand—and suddenly it cools off.

Many with the sparkling personalities have come into our churches—but most of them have done their sparkling and are gone.

The Holy Spirit, my brethren, rules out all of this sparkle and charm and pulpit presence and personal magnetism. Instead, He whispers to us: "God wants to humble you and fill you with Himself and control you so that you can become part of the eternal work that God wants to do in the earth in your day!"

Now, brethren, a word of encouragement. Just be-

41

cause the true gifts of the Spirit are so rare among us does not mean that they are missing entirely.

There has never been a time in the history of the Christian church that some of the gifts were not present and effective. Sometimes they have functioned even among those who did not understand or perhaps did not believe in the same way that we think Christians should believe. But the churches have prevailed and the faithful have been true to Christ. Link upon link, a chain of spiritual Christianity in consecutive linkage has been fashioned by the Holy Spirit!

What we do for God must be done in the power of the Holy Spirit and we know that we may have little praise from men. But what we do accomplish for Him as true spiritual work done with eternity in view will have His praise written across it: "This came to live and to last!"

Most of us have never heard—or do not remember—the name of the humble 16-year-old girl whose singing ministry brought such spiritual results in the Welsh revivals with Evan Roberts.

This quiet, humble girl would sing the gospel songs even though the singing of solos was not regularly a part of their services. They sang in choral groups and they used the metric psalter which did not particularly lend itself to solo expression.

Much has been said about the young woman's spiritual gift—the Spirit-given ability to glorify the Saviour when she would rise to sing. Not too much has been said about her voice. I do not know how much lyrical beauty or quality was in her voice, but the record is clear that she was a gifted soul—that the Holy Spirit seemed to be singing and moving through her yielded expression.

42

When she sang about the Lord Jesus Christ and the plan of salvation, the goodness and mercy of God and the need of all for the Saviour, the hearts of men and women in the audience melted and the Spirit brought His conviction.

Evan Roberts would rise to preach and there was little left for him to do. He said that he would quote from the Scriptures and add an exhortation, and the people were ready to come to Christ. She had melted them with the warmth and power of the Spirit—she humbly exercised the unusual gift which God had bestowed.

It was not just a local incident. Wherever she went to sing for the Lord, the results were the same.

Oh, what we would be tempted to do with her ministry in this day! We would put her on the radio and show off her talent—and spoil her. Thank God that they knew better than to start writing her life history. Thank God she was not pressed into writing a tract: "My Life—from Nursery to Pulpit!"

She was a beautiful example of what we have been pleading for—the humble use of our spiritual gifts for the glory of Jesus Christ. She was a simple Welsh girl —willingly controlled by the Holy Spirit of God. As far as I know, there was never a music critic anywhere that ever said she had a good voice—but she had something far better!

The Holy Spirit is the gentle dove of God and His coming to us in blessing and power is without pain or strain. The painful part is the necessity of our own preparation—for the Holy Spirit will search us out completely and deal with us solemnly.

He will guide us in necessary confessions that we must make. He will guide us in the necessity of pouring out all of that which is selfish and unlike Jesus in our lives. He will guide us in getting straightened out with people with whom we have had differences. He will guide us in seeking forgiveness where it is necessary and He will show us the necessity of old-fashioned restitution and restoration in our willingness to be a clean vessel.

Plainly I can say that some folks who carry their big Bibles to impress others will never be filled with the Holy Spirit until they drop their sleek, smooth exterior of being "well taught" and earnestly desire God's humble plan for their lives.

After the desire must come a determination to go through with God on His terms—and even then, they will not be filled and owned and controlled by the Spirit of God until in desperation they throw themselves into the arms of God!

In the desire of our faith, we have to close our eyes and make a leap into the arms of Jesus! After all the help, after all the instructions, after all the study, after all the Bible verses you can remember have not done the work, after every trick and everything you know to move toward God have failed, your heart in desperation cries, "Fill me now! Oh, fill me now!"

Then you move into that zone of obscurity where the human reason has to be suspended for a moment and the human heart leaps across into the arms of God. It is then, I say, that man's talents, man's glory, man's duty and even man's favor all flow out into the darkness of yesterday. Suddenly, everything is God's glory and God's honor and God's beauty and God's Spirit in your heart! You have been broken and melted and finally filled with His mighty Spirit to such a degree that no man can change your mind!

I was nineteen years old, earnestly in prayer, kneeling in the front room of my mother-in-law's home, when I was baptized with a mighty infusion of the Holy Ghost. I had been eager for God's will and I had been up against almost all of the groups and "isms" with their formulas and theories and teachings.

They had all tried to beat me down. Some said I went too far and others said I had not gone far enough. But let me assure you, brethren, that I know with assurance what God did for me and within me and that nothing on the outside now held any important meaning. In desperation, and in faith, I took that leap away from everything that was unimportant to that which was most important—to be possessed by the Spirit of the Living God!

Any tiny work that God has ever done through me and through my ministry for Him dates back to that hour when I was filled with the Spirit. That is why I plead for the spiritual life of the Body of Christ and the eternal ministries of the Eternal Spirit through God's children—His instruments!

Chapter Four

No Second-Class Christians: The Church Still the Church

For as the body is one, and hath many members, and all the members of that one body, being many, are one body: so also is Christ. For by one Spirit are we all baptized into one body. . . . Now ye are the body of Christ, and members in particular. 1 Corinthians 12: 12-13, 27.

The eternal promises of Jesus Christ to His believing people are of such inestimable value that those who are truly Christian today are not to be designated as marginal or second-class Christians because of the passing of time and of generations gone before.

We are Christians because God has perpetuated the church and keeps it going by doing the same thing within individual lives generation after generation since Pentecost.

Do we believe as truth and claim it as we should that the true church as it meets in the Name to worship the Presence finds Christ still giving Himself in the life of the fellowship?

It is not the form that makes the church or its service. The Presence and the Name—these make the church.

Wherever people are gathered together in the Name, there also is the Presence. So it is that the Presence and the Name constitute the true assembly of believers and it is recognized by God in heaven.

In my estimation this brings to light a most wonderful truth! In the Body of Christ there are no insignificant congregations. Each has His Name and each is honored by His Presence.

It has been related that a young pastor commented when introduced to a well-known church leader: "Doctor, I am sure you don't know me. I am the pastor of just a little rural church."

I think it was a wise reply that came from that churchman: "Young man, there are no little churches; all churches are the same size in God's sight."

Large or small—it must be an assembly of believers brought together through a Name to worship a Presence. The blessed thing is that God does not ask whether it is a big church or a little church.

But people do insist on asking questions about the size and number of people in a church because they are carnal. I know all about such human judgments: "This is a very little church" or "That is a poor, unknown church."

Meanwhile, God is saying, "They are all My churches and each has every right to all that I bestow!"

I am of the opinion that every local church should be fully aware of its relationship to the church in the New Testament.

We should ask ourselves if we are as truly interested in spiritual attainment as were the New Testament believers. We must confess that the spiritual temperature among us may often be lower than in the early church. But we cannot escape the message that those who truly meet in His Name to honor the Presence of the Saviour are included in this relationship which goes back to the New Testament and to the apostles.

Consider with me some very serious thoughts about the fact that God works to perpetuate by repetition.

First, let us review how God keeps the human race going.

In every human being there is the strange, mysterious and sacred life stream which God created in Adam and Eve. This has been perpetuated throughout the centuries by constant repetition in each generation. It is the same human race with the same human nature. It simply repeats itself in every generation.

It is true that we who inhabit the earth today are not the same persons who inhabited the earth when Columbus discovered America. Not one individual living now was alive then. Nevertheless, it is the same race. God has activated the continuity of the human race by perpetuating each generation and repeating each generation through the mystery of life in procreation.

Israel is an illustration of this concept.

Israelites living at the time of Moses were not the same Israelites who lived in the time of David. It was, however, the same Israel by the mystery of repetition in procreation.

It was the same God, the same covenant, the same relationship, the same revelation, the same fathers, the same intention and purpose. It was the same nation.

That is why God could speak to Israel in Moses' day, in David's day, and in Christ's day, and be speaking to the same Israel. Actually it was the same Israel secured and perpetuated in unbroken continuity by the creative mystery of procreation and repetition.

I believe that it is exactly the same with the church of our Lord Jesus Christ—the true church that is alive today.

In this context I am not referring to lifeless churches and unbelieving churches. I have in mind the true churches, the assemblies of faithful believers.

The personnel is not the same as in the days when Wesley preached. When Wesley preached, there was not one person who was alive when Luther preached. When Luther preached, there was not a man or woman remaining of those who lived when Bernard, the ancient saint, wrote his great hymns.

My point is that each generation has different personnel, but it is the same church which comes down in unbroken lineal descent from that earliest church.

You and I confess that we are not the same as Adam nor are we the same as Adam's grandchildren or great-great-great grandchildren. Nevertheless, we contend that we are truly related to him as were his sons, Cain and Abel—all being related to him by the mystery of procreation and the continuity of life that solidifies and holds together in one the human race.

I think it should be plain that the truth concerning the on-going life of the Christian church is not the same as the continuing historical progression of national life.

There is only a political unity that can be achieved in a nation. The British empire existed through its many generations by means of a political unity. But it is not a political unity that holds the human race together—it is a biological unity, the life stream that makes it one.

Regardless of how you break up the human race into political parties and distinctions it is still one by the mystery of perpetuated life.

So it is with the church of Christ. It has never been the political organization or segments that hold it together. When we talk about our Protestant tradition—the tradition of the fathers—we talk metaphorically and beautifully. But we do not mean the same thing that I mean when I say that a local assembly of faithful believers is in straight biological lineal descent from the apostles!

That is not political nor ideological but biological. It has to do with the mystery of life. It has to do with the life of God in man—the Holy Ghost doing in men of our day what He did in men of long ago.

While I thank God in appreciation for all of the great and godly men in the history of the church, we actually follow none of them. Our charter goes farther back and is from a higher source. They were looked upon as leaders, but they were all servants even as you and I are.

Luther sowed, Wesley watered, Finney reaped, but they were only servants of the living God.

In our local assemblies we are part of the church founded by the Lord Jesus Christ and perpetuated by the mystery of the new birth. Therefore our assembly is that of Christian believers gathered unto a Name to worship and adore that Presence.

If this is true—and everything within me witnesses that it is—all the strain is gone. I mean the strain is gone even about traditional religious forms—the pressures that we must sing certain songs, recite certain prayers and creeds, follow accepted patterns in ministerial leadership and service. All of these begin to pale in importance as we function in faith as the people of God who glorify the Name that is above every name and honor His Presence!

Yes, I contend that He is able to do for us all that He did in the days of the apostles. Oh, the power that is ours—the potential that we possess because He is here. Our franchise still stands! There has been no revocation of our charter!

If a poll should be taken today to name the six greatest men in the world and our names would not be included, we would still have the same privileges in God's world that they would have! We can breathe God's beautiful air, look at His blue sky, gaze into a never-ending array of stars in the night sky. We can stand upon the hard earth and stamp our little feet— and our big feet, too—and know that it will sustain us. We are as much a part of this human race as the greatest men and women.

And spiritually there is no blessing or privilege ever given by God that is withheld from us today—understanding, of course, that we know what the Bible really says.

For instance, we know that we cannot have the new heavens and the new earth right now although we can have the essence of them in our beings now.

We also know that right now we cannot have the

new body that God is going to give at the coming of Christ.

But all things that are for us now we can have, and it is easy to find out what they are!

Why is it, then, that believers are not experiencing all that God desires for them? Why is it that our church attendance has become a social thing? Why does it become merely form and ritual?

Well, it is because we are badly instructed. We have been badly taught.

We have been told that we are a different kind of religion now and have been since the passing of the apostles.

"This is a different age in the church. The devil is busy and we cannot have and know and experience what they had then," we are told.

I have a strong reaction to that kind of teaching. I believe that any person who dares to say that is in the same position as a man who refuses to let your children open your own pantry door and refuses to let them sit down at your table.

Any kind of teaching or exposition, so called, that shuts us out from the privileges and promises of the New Testament is wrong, and the man who tries to shut me out is a false teacher!

Who gave any man the right to stand at your dining room table when your wife announces that dinner is ready and not let your children partake of the meal?

Who has the right in the name of bad teaching to keep your children away from your table? They are your children and you are responsible for them. You have an unwritten covenant with them and that table is spread for them. You may reserve the right to tell them how they should behave, but no one has the right to shut them out.

Let me ask the question: what right has any man to tell me, in the name of Bible teaching, that I belong to a different church than that early church?

Who should tell me that the fire has dimmed down in glory and that the mighty arm of God's Christ is now a diminished power?

When I am reading my New Testament, who can say, "But this portion is not for you. That portion is not for you. That promise is not for you"?

Who has been given the right to stand thus at the door to the kingdom of God?

Nobody!

Any kind of teaching or exposition, so called, that shuts me out from the privileges and promises of the New Testament is wrong. The man who tries to do so is a false teacher.

Another very evident reason why we do not receive as much from God as we should is because of the general low level of spiritual enthusiasm and the chilling effect of bad examples.

We would be foolish to try to deny that there are bad examples in our Christian circles.

I hope that we will never go into panic because someone cynical declares: "I repudiate the Christian church because of all the bad things I know about certain congregations!"

There are always pretenders. We have all heard of instances of fleshly extravagances among professing followers of Christ. It cannot be denied that such behavior is always a hindrance to the faith—and discourages faithfulness on the part of others.

Now, bad examples are one thing—but would we

repudiate the twelve apostles because there was a Judas? the thousands because there was an Ananias and a Sapphira? Would we repudiate Paul because there was a Demas?

I say certainly not!

I will not repudiate the assembly of the saints because a bad example shows up occasionally.

I doubt that any one of us following the Lord has been so perfect that he could claim he had never been a bad or wrong example.

But this is what our Christian gospel and the victorious life in the Body of Christ is all about!

It is the blood of the everlasting covenant that makes the sinner clean and makes the weak strong, providing forgiveness and justification through God's mercy and grace.

What God has made clean let us never call unclean! There is a fountain filled with blood—and whatever the child of God's past, his present life is revealed by the Spirit of God as a beautiful gift from God shining as a witness for the Saviour in the fellowship of the body.

Christ sealed that eternal covenant of grace with His blood when He gave Himself on the cross. It is a covenant that cannot be broken. It is a covenant that has never been amended or edited or altered. It is an effective truth that the power and the provisions, the promises and gifts that marked that early church can belong to us now.

If we will let Him, Christ will do in us and through us that which He did in and through the committed believers after Pentecost.

The potential is ours. Do we dare believe that the

faithful Christian believers may yet experience a great new wave of spiritual power?

It probably will not come across the wide, broad church with its amusements and worldly nonsense, but it will surely come to those who desire the presence and blessing of God more than they want anything else!

It will come to the humble, faithful, and devoted believers whoever and wherever they are!

I confess I want to be in such a spiritual condition that I may share in God's blessings as they come, no matter what the cost may be.

I want you as followers of Christ and in lineal descent from the apostles who meet regularly in His Name to honor His Presence to share in all the revelation of His fullness.

To miss out in any degree of all that God provides for us is tragedy—pure and simple.

No Christian can afford to miss God's best!

Chapter Five

An Assembly of Saints: Love Unity in the Spirit

But now hath God set the members every one of them in the body, as it hath pleased him . . . having given more abundant honour to that part which lacked: That there should be no schism in the body; . . . Now ye are the body of Christ, and members in particular. 1 Corinthians 12:18, 24-25, 27

Stating it in just about the most simple terms we know, the Christian church is the assembly of redeemed saints.

And stating it in what is probably the most important teaching in the New Testament concerning Christ and the church, Paul pointedly relates the life and service of the Christian church to a true unity which can only be wrought by the Holy Spirit!

Paul wrote specifically to the first century Corinthian believers to remind them that "as the body is one, and hath many members, and all the members of that one body, being many, are one body: so also is Christ."

Then he continued: "For by one Spirit are we all baptized into one body, whether we be Jews or Gentiles, whether we be bond or free; and have been all made to drink into one Spirit. For the body is not one member, but many" (1 Cor. 12:12-14).

Now, in our local church or assembly, we know that we are not an end in ourselves. We want to see the church, the Body of Christ, as a whole. If we are going to be what we ought to be in the local church, we must come to think of ourselves as a part of something more expansive, something larger that God is doing throughout the entire world.

There is an important sense here in which we find that we "belong"—belonging to something that God has brought into being, something that is worthy and valuable, and something that is going to last forever.

We do not have to be ashamed as redeemed men and women that we desire to belong to the work that God is doing through the church.

You know, sociologists and psychologists talk about the need for belonging. They tell us that a rejected child, one who no longer belongs to anyone, will develop dangerous mental and nervous traits.

They tell us that the wolf packs—the neighborhood clubs of young boys and girls who roam and terrorize the streets—come largely from homes where they have been rejected. Many young children in our day cannot remember ever having been loved by a mother or a father, and so they come together and find some answer to their own need in belonging to a gang.

These young people and many others in every walk of life have found a new sense of human strength in their "belonging" to others. That is the reason there are many popular secret orders and societies. Men who are pushed around by their wives and submerged and humiliated by their superiors at work soon get the feeling that they have no soul to call their own. Because they need some point at which to rally their self-respect they join a lodge or fraternal society—and they "belong" to something.

Perhaps you saw the recent cartoon in which the wife blocked the doorway and said to the husband: "The high exalted potentate can't go out tonight because I won't let him!"

The point is that little men want to belong to something and that is basically not a bad thing because we are gregarious by nature.

We are not wolves, to go alone or travel in narrow packs which break up immediately.

No. Actually, we are sheep. Sheep travel together in flocks and stay together for a lifetime.

We are thinking together here about the whole church, the Body of Christ, and the fact that in our local congregation we have the joyful sense of belonging to an amazing fellowship of the redeemed throughout the world.

This is entirely different from belonging to an order or a society or a group that is man-made.

Most of you know that God made my knees hard to bend, and I am sure you have never imagined me getting on my knees and swearing to follow some order of this or some secret society of that. My American upbringing has made it almost impossible to bend my knees in that regard—unless God bends them!

But I am not ashamed that I want to belong to something good and great and eternal—for no man is ever individually big enough to go it alone.

No man—unless he is sick. The hermit, for instance, is sick. The man who lives alone in his attic, refusing to answer the door, sneaking out in the dark to buy a little food—that man is sick. He is not a normal man.

A normal man, good or bad, sinner or saint, wants to walk out and look around at others of his kind with the inward feeling: "I belong. This is my race. These are my people. This is my language being spoken. That's my flag there on top of the school building. I belong here!"

That is a kind of personality thing that is necessary to our human welfare—necessary to our health, our mental health.

And that is why unwanted children and other persons who feel themselves rejected may develop serious and dangerous behavior trends.

That's why we enjoy singing songs about the church—because we have come to think of ourselves in relationship to the whole church of Christ.

Our hymns repeat with meaning that we are the church, the redeemed, and that Jesus Christ purchased us with His own blood. We are the church, now part in heaven and part on earth, and of "every color and tribe and nation and tongue around the world," as the Bible teaches.

Thankfully, we are a part of that!

I dare to say to you that we did not get our beginning when Dr. A. B. Simpson organized the society for Christian missions in New York City in 1884. If I thought for a second that that was our beginning, I would never finish this sentence. I would just break it off with a semi-colon. I would close the Bible and leave the pulpit and resign.

But I believe that we are a part of that great Christian body that goes back to Pentecost. I believe in a true kind of apostolic succession, not a succession of bishops and men with names and organizations, but a living organism vitally a part of the true church of Christ that began when the Holy Ghost came upon a body of believers and made them one, making them God's people in a way that none ever had been before!

This is an important Biblical concept—that every believing Christian has a part with us and we have a part with every faithful Christian group throughout the world!

This is so true that when I hear of some good thing that has been said or done by a good man or woman anywhere in the world for the sake of Christ's gospel, I have a good feeling in my heart. That has become a part of me—that belongs to me, and I have a part in it. It doesn't matter whether I will ever personally meet that person on earth, for the church of our Lord Jesus Christ is one.

Now, I want to think of you and your relation to God first of all.

A minister got his name in the papers here by starting a campaign to get all the members of his church to vote.

As your pastor, just let me say that I expect you to vote as a good Christian citizen, but that's your own business. If you do not vote, I am not going to needle you about that. I can only remind you that every nation pretty much gets the kind of leaders it deserves.

This is what I mean: I am more deeply concerned

about your relationship to God and your continuing spiritual life than I am about a campaign to get you out to the polls. Before there were any Tories or Whigs or Democrats or Republicans or Socialists or Christian Fronts—there was God! And before men and women ever knew the privilege of the ballot—there was God.

There is no doubt in my mind that your relationship to God is the matter that must come first— absolutely!

Then your relationship to others may be next in importance, followed by such things as your service for our Lord and your habits of life.

What about prayer and its meaning in our Christian fellowship?

It is my belief that it is a high Christian privilege to pray for our own congregation and then to pray for other believers throughout the Christian church.

Speaking as a minister it is my strong feeling that no man has a right to preach to a crowd that he has not prayed for.

Some people want to shy away from the word *duty*, but nevertheless I believe I have a duty and a responsibility to pray for those who are striving to walk with God in the fellowship of the church.

Just this word about duty: a frisky young colt in the pasture knows nothing about anything that could be called duty. But that colt's well-trained, hardworking mother in the harness and pulling a wagon or plow is an example of fulfilling the implications of duty.

The colt only knows freedom, but the work horse knows duty.

I cannot help but wonder if our inordinate desire for freedom and our strange fear of duty have had an effect upon the life of the church. We ought to consider it a privilege as well as a sacred duty to pray for our church and for others who are included in the fellowship of the Christian faith.

I know that there are people who attend churches where there is never any appeal or desire to engage in effectual prayer for others. They can tell you the name of their church and when it was organized and what part it plays in the "religious community."

That's not enough. Strictly speaking, you cannot bring a true segment of the Body of Christ into being by organizing.

Now I do not want to be misquoted. I believe that within our Christian fellowship and in our efforts to evangelize there must of necessity be some proper organization freely exercised. Paul himself must have had this in mind as he wrote to Titus and told him to set things in order and to appoint men to tasks within the fellowship.

But I am saying that you cannot organize a Christian church in the same way that you would organize a baseball club. In baseball you need a captain, so many pitchers and so many catchers, outfielders and infielders and a number of coaches.

You can have an organized ball club with the right number of players and coaches and still not have a ball club, as a certain Chicago team has proven!

No, you cannot organize a true Christian church in that sense. Even after the adoption of a proper church constitution there may not actually be a New Testament church. Perhaps the church is within that organization—it is possible—but that organization is not the church, for the church is the assembly of the saints!

No congregation or church group has the right to feel that it has finally arrived and is fully matured. Every congregation with a true desire for the knowledge of God must continually seek and reach out— determining its own needs and what it should be to be well pleasing to the Lord.

Any assembly of the saints must continue in the study of the Bible to determine what the Holy Spirit wants to do in the life of the church and how the Spirit will provide the power and special abilities to glorify Jesus Christ.

You will know what I mean when I say that to do all this requires in itself a gift of the Spirit!

Let me here refer to words of the prophet Isaiah which I love very much. They are in Isaiah chapter 11:

"And there shall come forth a rod out of the stem of Jesse, and a Branch shall grow out of his roots: and the spirit of the Lord shall rest upon him, the spirit of wisdom and understanding, the spirit of counsel and might, the spirit of knowledge and of the fear of the Lord; and shall make him of quick understanding in the fear of the Lord: and he shall not judge after the sight of his eyes, neither reprove after the hearing of his ears: but with righteousness shall he judge the poor, and reprove with equity for the meek of the earth" (vv. 1-4a).

Now as you well know all of that was spoken by the prophet concerning Jesus, the One who was to come to Israel.

But don't you think that description of spiritual life and ministry also should be true of all who are members of the Body of Christ by faith?

Just as in the Old Testament when the oil of anointing was poured out on the high priest's head and ran down to the skirt of his garment and on down to his feet, giving fragrance and sweetness to his whole body, so the mighty power that was poured upon the head of Jesus must flow and trickle down to every member of the body. What was true of Him, our Lord, can just as surely be true of those who minister His grace and truth.

"The spirit of wisdom and understanding, the spirit of counsel and might, the spirit of knowledge and of the fear of [Jehovah]; and shall make him of quick understanding . . . and he shall not judge after the sight of his eyes" (vv. 2-3).

What a powerful message from the prophet to our own day. The curse of modern Christian leadership is the pattern of looking around and taking our spiritual bearing from what we see, rather than from what the Lord has said.

"Neither [shall he] reprove after the hearing of his ears" (v. 3).

But what are we prone to do in church leadership? We are likely to listen carefully to see which way things are moving and then act accordingly. But the Spirit of God will never lead us into that mistake.

"But with righteousness shall he judge the poor, and reprove with equity for the meek of the earth. . . . And righteousness shall be the girdle of his loins, and faithfulness the girdle of his reins" (vv. 4a, 5).

Led by the Spirit of God, the members of the Body of Christ will always be right in their spirit, right in their wisdom, and right in their judgment. They will not be judged nor will they allow themselves to be judged on the basis of what is currently taking place all around them.

I believe God wants to do something new and

blessed for every believer who has the inner desire to know Him better. I am aware of the fact that it takes a store of patience and persistence and a lot of courage to find and pursue the will of God in this day. There has been a reviving within the ranks of our own fellowship, and I see no reason why it should not flow out and down and over and up and around until we are all swimming in it.

Brethren, we fellowship here and mingle together and worship the Lord Christ as an assembly of the saints. We confess that all of the privileges and responsibilities rest upon us that once rested upon those believers at Pentecost. The plan and promises of God for His believing children have not diminished one little bit.

Nowhere in the Word of God is there any text or passage or line that can be twisted or tortured into teaching that the organic living church of Jesus Christ just prior to His return will not have every right and every power and every obligation that she knew in that early part of the book of Acts.

I am determined that we are not going to give up to the kind of times in which we live! There is such a thing as just getting tough about this, my brethren. There is such a thing as saying in the power of the Spirit, "I am not yielding and I will not give up to the times!" This is something we can say to our Lord and to ourselves, and betimes, maybe, over our shoulder to the devil!

The faithful Body of Christ is not going to give up to the ways of the world or even to the more common ways of religion that we see all about us.

Faithful believers in Christ are not going to give

up to the temptation to judge themselves according to what others are doing.

Neither will they allow their church to be judged and its spiritual life to be affected by the attitudes of others. They will be happy and continue to rejoice in the fact that they have taken the New Testament standard as their standard in their Christian fellowship.

Believing Christians and the groups that trust and obey the Scriptures are now known generally as fundamentalists—and that's not bad. But I think we need a caution and a warning in our midst that it is not enough just to have the label of orthodox belief.

I really think that all of us who love our Lord Jesus Christ are facing such great changes in this period before the return of Christ that we are going to have to recall and have back upon us the kind of spiritual revival that will eventuate in a new moral power, in a new spirit of willing separation and heart purity, and a new bestowing of the enablings of the Spirit of God.

If we do not earnestly seek it and if we do not obtain it, it is my opinion that God will somehow raise up some new segment of the Body of Christ to carry the torch.

This is a prophecy that has little chance of contradiction in the kind of times in which we live. If we do not make a hard swing back to the very roots of Christian faith and Christian teaching and Christian living, beginning again to seek the face of God and His will, God is going to pass us up!

He will pass us up as a farmer deals with egg shells that are empty. He carries them out and buries them, as we bury the dead after the spirit has departed.

There was a day when leaders in Israel, believing

in the perpetuity of her place in the sun, said to Jesus, "We be not born of fornication. We be the seed of Abraham. And this temple is the temple of God."

And Jesus answered, "They are the children of Abraham who do the works of Abraham. As for this temple, there is coming a day when not one stone will be left upon another."

And that, of course, came to pass later when the Roman emperor sent his plows to raze the foundation and to separate all of the great temple stones. He had never heard those prophetic words of Jesus, but this was the means of fulfilling them in the program of God. It had been a sacred temple to the Jews—but the Roman conquerors knocked down every stone level with the ground.

God makes His moves in dealing with nations and men and with men's favorite religions and temples. There is no religious group or church organization or denominational communion in the world that God will not desert and abandon in the very hour it ceases to fulfill and carry out His divine will.

There is no possible way that ecclesiastical robes are impressive enough nor cross and chains heavy enough nor titles long enough to save the church when once she ceases to fulfill the will of God among sinful men who need the transforming news of Christ's gospel.

The God who raised them up in centuries past will turn away and abandon them unless they continue to fulfill the gracious will of God, following on to know the Lord, humbly and meekly in faith and in love.

I am talking about the crowd, now. Not the individual members. Just because some organization has a great crowd is not the significant issue with God. The

Lord will turn His blessing to some small mission, to simple-hearted people somewhere whose greatest possession is the desire to love God and to obey Him.

God never leaves or forsakes His believing children. But I surely believe that God has lifted the cloud and the fire of His presence from groups and assemblies that plainly forsook Him and His eternal Word.

And, dear God, I pray that if it ever lifts from this church, you will tell me 24 hours before the tragedy occurs—for I want to get out of town! I want time to get away where I won't have to stand and look at the despoiling of the church.

Oh, brethren, we may lack everything else, but we must have the cloud and fire of His presence; we must have the enabling and the power of the Holy Spirit and the glow of the Shekinah glory—God with us!

For then, even lacking everything else, you still have a true church!

Chapter Six

God's Eternal Purpose:
Christ, the Center of All Things

And as they thus spake, Jesus himself stood in the midst of them, and saith unto them, Peace be unto you. Luke 24:36

Contrary to the opinion held by many would-be religious leaders in the world, Christianity was never intended to be an "ethical system" with Jesus Christ at the head.

Our Lord did not come into the world 2,000 years ago to launch Christianity as a new religion or a new system. He came into this world with eternal purpose. He came as the center of all things. Actually, He came to be our religion, if you wish to put it that way.

He came in person, in the flesh, to be God's salvation to the very ends of the earth. He did not come just to delegate power to others to heal or cure or bless. He came to *be* the blessing, for all the blessings and the full glory of God are to be found in His person.

Because Jesus Christ is the center of all things, He offers deliverance for the human soul and mind by His direct, personal and intimate touch. This is not my one-man interpretation. It is the basic teaching of salvation through the Messiah-Saviour, Jesus Christ. It is a teaching that runs throughout the Bible!

I remind you that Jesus Christ came into a world of complex religious observances. Perhaps it can be likened to a kind of religious jungle, with a choking and confusing multiplicity of duties, rituals and observances laid upon the people. It was a jungle grown so thick with man-made ordinances that it brought only a continuing darkness.

Into the midst of all this came the Light that was able to light every man that was to come into the world. He could say and teach, "I am the light of the world," because He shone so brightly, dispelling the darkness.

Jesus Christ came in the fullness of time to be God's salvation. He was to be God's cure for all that was wrong with the human race.

He came to deliver us from our moral and spiritual disorders—but it must also be said He came to deliver us from our own remedies.

Religion as a form is one of the heaviest burdens that has ever been laid upon the human race, and we must observe that it is a self-medicating burden. Men and women who are conscious of their moral and spiritual disorders try to medicate themselves, hoping to get better by their own treatment.

I often wonder if there is any kind of self-cure or

human medication that man has not tried in his efforts to restore himself and gain merit.

Millions of pilgrims may still be seen in India, flat on the ground, crawling like inchworms toward the Ganges river, hoping for a release from the burden of guilt in the sacred waters.

History tells of countless persons who have tried to deal with guilt by self-denial and abstaining from food and drink. Many have tried a kind of self-torture by putting on hair shirts or walking on spikes or on hot coals. Men with the hermit complex have shunned society and hidden themselves in caves, hoping to gain some merit that would bring them closer to God and compensate for their own sinful nature.

Mankind is still inventing new ways of self-treatment and medication for failures and weaknesses and wrong-doing, even in our own day, not recognizing that the cure has already come.

Simeon, the old man of God who had waited in hope around the temple, knew that the cure had come! When he saw the baby Jesus, he took Him up in his arms, looked down at Him and said, "Lord, now lettest thou thy servant depart in peace . . . for mine eyes have seen thy salvation" (Luke 2:29-30).

So, I say to those who doubt or to those who are not instructed that it is Jesus Christ Himself that Christianity offers to you. I know that some churches are confused because of the introduction of human ideas, such as the self-medication idea, which has grown and expanded much like the proverbial mustard tree.

But, really, all Christianity offers is Jesus Christ the Lord, and Him alone—for He is enough! Your relation to Jesus Christ is really the all-important matter in this life.

That is both good news and bad news. It is good news for all who have met our Saviour and know Him intimately and personally. It is bad news for those who hope to get into heaven some other way!

Notice in the record that Jesus stood in the midst and said, "Peace be unto you."

Here is a beautiful explanation of the angels' words, "Peace on earth, good will to men." The angels could say that only because it was Jesus who was coming! He is our peace. I once had a wall motto which said, "He is our peace." Because of the coming of Jesus, the angels could announce, "Peace on earth."

This portion of Scripture illustrated Jesus' method of imparting health, directly and personally. It was Christ in the midst—at the center—and He could take that place because He is God, He is spirit, He is timeless, He is spaceless, He is supreme, He is all in all. Therefore, He could be at the center!

Here I borrow an illustration to stress the point that Christ is the center of all things. He is, as it were, the hub of a wheel around which everything revolves. Centuries ago someone said that Christ is like the hub and everything that has been created is on the rim of the wheel.

One of the old church fathers said, "Everything that exists is equally distant from Jesus and equally near to Him."

There is the hub in the middle of each wheel with spokes going out to the rim. Then, in the perfectly shaped wheel, the rim goes around equal distance at all points from the hub. To us, Jesus Christ is that hub and everything else is on the rim. When Jesus

Christ has His place as hub, we are all equally close or equally far from Him.

Jesus is in the midst, and because that is true, He is accessible from anywhere in life. This is good news—wonderful, good news!

This truth makes it possible for us to insist that Jesus Christ is at the center of geography. No one, therefore, can claim an advantage with Christ because of location.

It so happens that I am at the present time reading Neuman's *History of Latin Christianity* and have read again the story of the Crusaders. At the time of the historic crusade, many believed that merit was to be gained by making a pilgrimage to the very place where Jesus was born, and particularly to the sepulcher where His body was laid.

When Peter the Hermit, old and barefooted, whipped all of Europe into a white heat to get the crusades launched, he set the goal of liberating a grave out of which Jesus Christ had stepped more than a thousand years before. The crusaders felt that if that empty tomb could be taken from the Moslems, everything would be all right. Today there is still great interest in being where Jesus had been, but I don't know why we insist upon being spiritually obtuse.

Have we not heard Jesus' words: "I tell you that neither in this mountain nor in Jerusalem do men worship the Father, for the Father seeketh such to worship Him who worship Him in spirit and in truth" (see John 4:21-24). It is not on a certain mountain or in a city!

We wonder why the crusaders did not consider that. Why all the bloody wounds, starvation, suffering and death? Why the long, weary treks to get to the place where Jesus had been born or where He died, or where He had been buried? For there is no geographical advantage anywhere in the world. Not one of us would be a better Christian just by living in Jerusalem. If you lived at some spot in the world actually farther from Jerusalem, you would be at no disadvantage. Jesus Christ is in the very center of geography. It is just as near to Him from anywhere as it is from anywhere else! And it's just as far from Him also! So geography doesn't mean anything in our relationship to Him!

Plenty of money has been spent by preachers who felt that they could preach better if they could just visit Jerusalem. So they go over and look on Jerusalem, and when they come back, they have just a few more stories to tell. Actually, they are no better and their audiences are no better. Let's believe it—Jesus is the hub and geography is all around Him!

Then, we must come to the conclusion that Jesus Christ is the center of time. Many people become sad when they talk about missing the time of Christ on earth. It is good to recall and study the life and ministries of Jesus long ago. We sing a song that says: "I think when I read that sweet story of old, / When Jesus was here among men, / How He called little children as lambs to His fold, / I should like to have been with Him then!" Many a tear has been wiped out of the eyes when people have sung that, but did you know that the people who were with Jesus at the time when He walked among men were not as well off as they were ten days after He left them?

Ten days after He departed, He sent the Holy Spirit, and the disciples who understood only in part suddenly knew the plan of God as in a blaze of light.

But we say, "I would like to have lived in the time of Christ."

Why? There were hypocrites and Pharisees and opposers, murderers and unbelievers in the time of Christ! You would not have found things any better two thousand years ago.

Some of you who look back with nostalgia upon what you consider the good old days ought to be delivered from that!

Consider, too, that Jesus Christ is the center of the human race. With Him there are no favored races. We had better come to the point of believing that Jesus Christ is the Son of Man. He is not the Son of the first century nor the twentieth century. He is the Son of Man—not a Son of the Jewish race only. He is the Son of all races no matter what the color or tongue.

When Jesus Christ was incarnated in mortal flesh, He was not incarnated only in the body of the Jew, but in the body of the whole human race.

Go to Tibet or Afghanistan, to the Indians of South America, the Mohammedans of Arabia, the Englishmen of London, or the Scots of Glasgow and preach Jesus. If there is faith and willingness to follow, He will bring them all into His fellowship. They are all in the rim. They are all as near and all as far. That's the reason for the kind of missionary philosophy we hold. We do not first go into a country to educate the people and then preach Christ to them. We know better than that! We know that Jesus Christ is just as near to an uneducated, uncultured native as He is to a polished gentleman from New York or London.

Christ is at the center of all cultural levels. Preach Christ and show the love of God to the most primitive, most neglected, most illiterate people in the world; be patient and make them understand. Their hearts will awake, the Spirit will illuminate their minds. Those who believe on Jesus will be transformed. This is a beautiful thing that is being demonstrated over and over again in the world today.

In New Guinea and throughout parts of Indonesia, for instance, stone-age men and repulsive cannibals are being born again just as quickly as those with college degrees, because it is just as near to Jesus from the jungle as it is from the halls of ivy.

He is in the midst of all cultures!

Jesus is in the midst of all ages as well. By that I mean our human ages, our birthdays. It is just as near to Jesus at 80 years old as it is from eight; just as near from 70 as it is from seven.

We have been told that as we get older, we are harder to reach for God and the likelihood of our coming to Jesus diminishes. But our ability to come to Jesus— the distance we are from God—is no greater when we are 90 than when we were youngsters.

So, Jesus Christ stands in the middle of the human race, at the center of geography, the central figure in time, and in the midst of all cultures.

Our Lord is at the center of all life's experiences!

Our Lord speaks peace to us throughout life's experiences. An experience is awareness of things taking place around us. A newborn baby does not have experience. So far, he is just a little stranger in our world. But he learns fast, and very soon experience will teach him that when he howls, he will get attention.

The man who lives to be 100 years old has really had some experiences. However, if he lives somewhere in the hills and seldom comes out, he probably will have a narrow field of experience.

If he is a world traveler with a good education and a wide circle of friends, his experience will be so vast that it is a mystery as to how his brain can file away so much for future memory and reference.

I ask, which is nearer to Jesus? Does the child with little experience have an advantage over the man of wide experience? There is no difference! Jesus Christ stands in the middle of life's experiences and anyone can reach Him, no matter who he is!

Jonathan Edwards, that mighty preacher of the earlier days in our country, was converted when he was only five years old. He wrote, "I never backslid. I went right on." What experiences can a five-year-old boy have?

Read the early chapters of First Samuel and consider that the boy Samuel was twelve. He was just a lad. And then there was Eli, 98 years old. Here are the two of them—the boy and the aged man.

What experience had the boy had? Practically none. What experience had the old man had? Practically all. He had run the whole scale, the gamut of human possibilities. Yet it was just as near to God from young Samuel who had no experience as it was to Eli who had found out through the years what life was all about.

Remember that when our Lord hung on the cross, a superscription was written in Hebrew, Greek, and Latin and placed on the cross above His head: "This is Jesus Christ, the King of the Jews." Someone has pointed out that in doing this, God had taken in the whole world. Hebrew stands for religion; Greek for philosophy, and Latin for Rome's military prowess. All the possibilities of human experience on a world scale were taken in.

It was just as close from the Roman soldiers to the Son of God as from the Hebrew teacher, Nicodemus, who said, "Master, Thou art sent from God!"

So, the world of that day was really divided into three parts, and that is about all we have today, isn't it?

We still have religion, culture and the combination of military and politics. Everything else seems to fall somewhere inside those brackets.

Jesus Christ was crucified in the very center of man's world. So it is just as easy to reach Him from the philosopher's ivory tower as it is from the priest's sanctuary. It is just as easy for the uniformed soldier to reach Him as it is for the thinker with his big books.

Christ Jesus our Lord stands in the midst so no one can claim advantage. Thank God! No one can frighten me, intimidate me or send me away.

No one can put me down and say, "Ah, but you don't know!"

They have tried. They smile when they say it and I smile back and think, "Brother, you are the one who doesn't know—because I do know!"

I know that I can reach Him as quickly from where I am as any other man.

Einstein, with his great mind, could reach out and touch his Messiah if he would. There are many in America who cannot read or write. Einstein and the man who marks an X for his name are in the same category. Both are equal on the rim. No man can actually say that he has been given an advantage over others.

You say, then: "Why doesn't everybody come?"

Because of inexcusable stubbornness.

Because of unbelief.

Because of preoccupation with other things.

Because we do not believe that we really need Him!

Millions turn their backs on Him because they will not confess their need. If you have found you need Him, you can come to Him in faith, you can touch Him and feel His power flowing out to help you, whoever you are.

Jesus did not come to save learned men only. He came to save the sinner! Not white men only—but all colors that are under the sun. Not young people only—but people of all ages!

Let us believe that and let us honor Jesus in our midst! The most important thing about you and Jesus is that you can reach Him from where you are!

Chapter Seven

The Failing Believer:
God Has a Remedy

My little children, these things write I unto you, that ye sin not. And if any man sin, we have an advocate with the Father, Jesus Christ the righteous; And he is the propitiation for our sins; and not for our's only, but also for the sins of the whole world. 1 John 2:1-2

Although there is plain teaching throughout the Old and New Testaments concerning God's willingness to forgive and forget, there are segments of the Christian church which appear to be poorly taught concerning God's clear remedy through the atonement for the believer who has yielded to temptation and failed his Lord.

How important it is that we know how to encourage and deal with the distressed and guilt-ridden disciple who cries out in utter dejection and misery of soul: "I quit! I quit! It is no use. I am just worse than other people!"

Basically, why does God forgive sin?

Because God knows that sin is the dark shadow standing between Him and His highest creation, man. God is more willing to remove that shadow than we are to have it removed.

He wants to forgive us—and that desire is a part of His character.

The Word of God gives us the blessed authority to claim that all of God's believing children have a remedy and a sacrifice for the guilt of sin: "Bring your lamb! Bring your offering!"

In the Old Testament pattern of forgiveness, the Jew had to bring a lamb. In this church age, the New Testament Christian surely knows that he can bring no offering other than his trust in the eternal Lamb of God, offered once and forever efficacious!

By no stretch of the imagination can anyone claim that John was "excusing" sin in the writing of this important first epistle. Actually, his paragraphs bristle with condemnation of everything evil and certainly carry the message of a sin-hating God.

But under the inspiration of the Holy Spirit, John takes the position of a realist and indicates what our Lord has done to make it possible for weak and vacillating believers to find forgiveness and assurance in their daily experiences.

The apostle is not suggesting some theoretical posture for believers. He is taking things as he found them and dealing with them on the basis of their reality— and not theorizing on how they should have been.

John was a father in the Christian faith and had wide experience with human beings, particularly with redeemed human beings. With the Holy Spirit's guidance, the old apostle provides us with the truth that Christian believers should be aware of their need to depend upon the Lord moment by moment—for during our lifetime there will never be a time when there will not be at least a possibility of sinning!

John's language cannot be interpreted as encouragement for those in the kingdom of God to sin carelessly and willfully.

Here is an illustration that comes to my mind when I consider this portion of Scripture.

It is a common thing to find clinics and infirmaries within the great manufacturing and industrial complexes in metropolitan areas of our nation. Would you say that providing these services means that the companies involved are encouraging accidents and illnesses?

Recognizing the human situation, the companies build the clinics because the statistics indicate just about how many accidents and sicknesses will occur among the given number of people every year.

No, John's teaching is not an encouragement to sin. It might be considered a kind of spiritual clinic that extends a caution: "Watch out and do not sin. But if any man sin, he does have an advocate with the Father."

That advocate, that representative is Jesus Christ, the Righteous One, John continues, with the assurance that He is the propitiation for our sins, and then adds a beautiful, expansive parenthesis, "Not for ours only, but also for the sins of the whole world" (1 John 2:2).

Now it would be well to note that this "clinic" idea was actually instituted and carried out in Old Testament times.

I want to take you back into the fourth chapter of

Leviticus to connect the Old and New Testament plans of forgiveness, to show that the same Holy Spirit provided the inspiration throughout and that it is the same eternal Christ shining through every page and every chapter.

In this passage in Leviticus, there was a spiritual "clinic" provided for the people of Israel and for congregations that had become infected with evil and wrongdoing. Perhaps those who have neglected the Old Testament will be surprised to learn that even in that period of the Law, God promised and offered an immediate and efficacious remedy for those who fell short of His commands.

Notice what they were told to do about sin in Leviticus:

"If a soul shall sin through ignorance against any of the commandments of the Lord concerning things which ought not to be done, and shall do against any of them . . ." (4:2), there is a remedy for that man.

First, think with me about this phrase indicating that some wrongs may be done through ignorance.

I do not think the words *through ignorance* should cause you to picture in your mind a starry-eyed, honest-hearted person who just happened to sin accidentally. I think in realism we must face up to the fact here is a careless soul, one who has perhaps neglected the Scriptures and neglected to hear the Word of the Lord, and following the intent of his own heart has sinned against the commandments of the Lord.

But, thankfully, there is a remedy for him. God cares about him!

Continuing in this section of Leviticus, God's remedy for sin and wrongdoing was provided for several categories of persons within Israel.

We are told of the possibility of sin even among those who were the anointed priests of God.

I wish that did not have to be in the record—but I am glad it is. They were men and they were not perfect.

I have read something of the life of the godly Saint Theresa, who confessed that she felt that she was the least of all Christians, because she read of Christ's great saints before her time who began to live so earnestly for God immediately after they were converted that they no longer caused Him any grief by sinning.

And she said: "I cannot say that. I have to admit that I grieved God after I was converted and that makes me less than they."

That was a humble and very touching way to put it, but I think if the truth were known about any of the saints of God, Theresa's confession would be their confession, too!

Brethren, I wish it were possible to anoint the head of every Christian preacher so that he would never sin again while the world stands. Perhaps some would consider that a happy way to deal with the subject— but if any man can be removed from the possibility of sin, he can only be some kind of robot run by pulleys, wheels and pushbuttons, morally incapable of doing evil and, by the same token, morally incapable of doing good.

This squares with what I have always preached in this pulpit: if man's will is not free to do evil, it is not free to do good!

The freedom of human will is necessary to the concept of morality.

That is why I have not accepted the doctrine that our Lord Jesus Christ could not have sinned. If He could not have sinned, then the temptation in the wilderness was a grand hoax and God was a party to it!

Certainly as a human being He could have sinned, but the fact that He would not sin was what made Him the holy man He was.

On that basis, then, it is not the inability to sin but it is the unwillingness to sin that makes a man holy.

The holy man is not one who cannot sin.

A holy man is one who will not sin.

A truthful man is not a man who cannot talk. He is a man who can talk and he could lie, but he will not.

An honest man is not a man who is in jail where he cannot be dishonest. An honest man is a man who is free to be dishonest, but he will not be dishonest.

But returning to the Old Testament priest—there was a possibility that he would sin and be found standing in need of God's remedy.

He was an anointed priest, set apart to serve his fellowmen and represent them before the Lord. But if there were no possibility that he could sin and he was nothing more than a robot, he would never understand the needs and the guilt of his people.

He never could have known their difficulties and troubles.

A physician who himself had never felt any pain surely could never sympathize with an ailing, suffering patient.

Now, in Leviticus, what was the sinning priest to do? Should he give up to discouragement and gloom and failure?

The answer is no: there is a remedy!

And what about ministers and all of God's servants today? In a time of temptation and weakness and failure, do they just quit? Do they write a resignation and walk out, saying, "I am not an Augustine nor a Wesley nor a Simpson—therefore I will give up."

If they know the Word of God, they seek God's remedy.

The remedy in the Old Testament was clear and plain: "Let him bring for his sin, which he hath sinned, a young bullock without blemish unto the Lord for a sin-offering, and he shall bring the bullock unto the door of the tabernacle of the congregation before the Lord; and shall lay his hand upon the bullock's head, and kill the bullock before the Lord. And the priest that is anointed shall take of the bullock's blood, and bring it to the tabernacle of the congregation: and the priest shall dip his finger in the blood, and sprinkle of the blood seven times before the Lord, before the vail of the sanctuary. And the priest shall put some of the blood upon the horns of the altar of sweet incense before the Lord, which is in the tabernacle of the congregation; and shall pour all the blood of the bullock at the bottom of the altar of the burnt-offering, which is at the door of the tabernacle of the congregation" (Lev. 4:3-7).

Now, there you have atonement for sin in the Old Testament. The Lord our God was providing a day-by-day remedy for spiritual weakness and failure.

The next category of sinners in Leviticus was the entire assembly or congregation of Israel.

"If the whole congregation of Israel sin through ignorance, and the thing be hid from the eyes of the assembly, and they have done somewhat against any of the commandments of the Lord concerning things which should not be done, and are guilty; when the sin, which they have sinned against it, is known, then the congregation shall offer a young bullock for the sin"

(4:13-14), going through the same process of sacrifice for atonement.

Then Moses recorded the result of God's remedy: "And the priest shall make an atonement for them, and it shall be forgiven them" (4:20).

There was another category of men said to be in need of the remedy—the rulers who have sinned and done somewhat against the Lord.

The crux of all these instructions in Leviticus brings us to identification with a needy but blessed group— the common people!

"If any one of the common people sin through ignorance, while he doeth somewhat against any of the commandments of the Lord concerning things which ought not to be done, and be guilty; or if his sin, which he hath sinned, comes to his knowledge; then he shall bring his offering . . ." (4:27-28).

I think the reference to "if his sin comes to his knowledge" speaks of his conscience awaking to the fact that he has sinned. We read in the Gospels of the willful prodigal who left his father and went into a far country. But at last he came to himself, and acknowledged his guilt. Prior to that awakening, he had been just as thoroughly a sinner but would not confess it or acknowledge it.

I delight in these instructions of the Lord to the common people, and when I say I love the common people, I do not mean "common" in the sense of ugliness, ignorance, crudeness or vulgarity. But when I think of the common people so much loved by our Lord Jesus, I think of people like you and me. We make up that great throng of folks who are entirely without fame; we probably will never have our names in "Who's

Who" and we may never win the international peace or science or literature prize awards.

But we are the plain people—just the great multitude of common folks that God made!

When we look at a prize chrysanthemum in a flower show or florist's window, we are astonished at the beauty of the bloom. A lot of professional help goes into the making of a chrysanthemum. But for simple, plain people, I recommend a wide expanse of daisies or a great field of goldenrod nodding in the balmy, autumn sun. They are among the common flowers, plain and simple blooms—and they don't have an artificial price tag.

Also, a goldenrod doesn't require anything but God's spacious heaven above and His bright sunshine and space in which to grow. It will nod there in all its natural beauty, together with the yellow and white daisies and the black-eyed susans. They will all be there. They had their place centuries ago, and they will still be there in centuries to come, if the Lord tarries. They don't require much—they are the common flowers!

I believe there's more joy in discovering a common wild flower in the spring when you are scarcely expecting it than in paying inflated dollars for a bouquet of flowers that have been carefully tended by horticulturists.

Now that is not to speak against nice flowers—I like them all! But sometimes I wonder if they are worth all they cost. The common field flower costs nothing—just the effort to see it, that's all.

In the spiritual life, God has His chrysanthemums, I guess. We read the stories of the great saints, and I am a great admirer of every one of them. Perhaps in the long run I am more at home with God's common daisy varieties than I am with the great, carefully cultivated churchmen who have been His showpieces for centuries past. Wouldn't it be tragic if we had to say, "Now, God, we just have a few that we can call to your attention. We will give you Paul and Chrysostom and Augustine and Francis, and we will add Knox and Luther and Wesley, and that's about all we can muster."

God would smile and say, "No, those are just my prize chrysanthemums. They were some of the great fellows, with more potential, somehow. I am glad for every one of them, but I am not so poverty stricken for spiritual leadership that I need say I have no others."

Behold, gaze, look . . . see an innumerable company that no man can number—nodding, common flowers of field and meadow that just somehow took root and grew in the sunshine and looked heavenward and gathered the rain and the dew and loved God for His own sake.

They were men and women whose hands may have been grimy, and they perhaps did not understand all the learned illusions of the highly-educated preacher. They may have no degrees, but they form a great company, and they have the blessed marks of the family. The family resemblance is upon them. They belong to God. They may have grown up in an atmosphere where they had no opportunity to cultivate themselves as others did, but they were true to God in their day. These are the plain people with whom many authors have been intrigued—the simple, mute, unknown millions, the plain people willing to share their fragrance even in the desert places. That's my crowd—all the time—that's my crowd!

When I am with men known as "big preachers," I sit down and talk with them when they are willing. If we can talk about God or faith or good books, we hit it off for awhile. But mostly I wander off and hunt up some butcher from Atlanta or a carpenter from Detroit, perhaps a rubber worker from Akron, a machinist from Minneapolis or a small-time farmer from Ottumwa. I feel more at home among them because they are God's plain people, God's common people, and there are so many more of them.

Well, back to Leviticus!

If any one of the common people sin through ignorance, the Lord instructed, while he doeth somewhat against any of the commandments of the Lord concerning things which ought not to be done and be guilty, there is a remedy!

In this gathering of believers, it could be that some of us common people have sinned. I trust that we will let the Holy Spirit bring it to our knowledge and that we will not be careless about it. If it comes to our knowledge, and we know that we have sinned somewhat against any of the commandments of the Lord concerning things that ought not to be done, then what shall we do?

Shall we give in to discouragement and guilt and say, "I cannot be a Christian! It is impossible! The world is too tough! There is too much temptation! I am too weak! I am too busy! I cannot make any progress!"

No! There is a remedy in the atonement. It says, "Let him bring his offering; let him bring his offering . . ."

An offering has already been provided. It does not mean that you should bring your money. No, no man of God will ever trick you like that—God forbid! I would live on rolled oats the rest of my life before I would identify any gift to the church with the offering of the Lamb of God!

But, bring your offering! Your offering has already been made: "Behold the lamb of God who beareth away the sin of the world!" You do not have to search for a lamb. Your sacrifice has been made once and is efficacious forever!

> Not all the blood of beasts on Jewish altars slain
> Could give the guilty conscience peace, or wash
>   away the stain.
> But Christ, the heavenly Lamb, takes all our
>   sins away;
> A sacrifice of nobler name and richer blood than
>   they!

Continuing, Isaac Watts, that man of God, confessed,

> My faith would lay her hand on that dear head
>   of Thine;
> While like a penitent I stand, and there confess
>   my sin.
> My soul looks back to see the burden Thou didst
>   bear,
> When hanging on the accursed tree, and knows
>   her guilt was there!

So in the covenant of grace, you need only lay your hand upon the head of the sin offering, the Lamb which was provided!

Oh, what does that mean to us? It means identification.

In the New Testament there is much said about the

laying on of hands. It was symbolic of identification and union.

We lay our hands on the head of a young minister being ordained as we identify ourselves with him and with others who laid their hands on our heads, a holy succession through the years.

The one who recognized his guilt was to lay his hands on the head of the offering in the Old Testament plan—thus identifying himself with the offering of sacrifice. That common man who had sinned was saying, "Oh, God, I deserve to die. Through faith in the mystery of atonement, I am going to live and this lamb will die. I lay my hand on his head, confess my sins, and my sins will be laid upon the lamb, as it were."

In the sacrificial death of the lamb, God was telling us that one day a perfect Lamb would come who would not merely symbolically take away sin, but would actually take away sin, because His blood would be richer and His name would be nobler.

He—Jesus—is the propitiation for our sins and for the sins of the whole world.

Sometimes when I am alone with my Bible, I get on my knees and turn to Isaiah 53. For every pronoun there I put all three of my names in. Then I read it aloud.

"Surely he hath borne Aiden Wilson Tozer's griefs, and carried Aiden Wilson Tozer's sorrows: . . . He was wounded for Aiden Wilson Tozer's transgressions, he was bruised for Aiden Wilson Tozer's iniquities."

That is laying your hand on the head of the sacrifice and identifying yourself with the dying lamb.

You can do that today!

Chapter Eight

The Resurrection of Christ: More Than a Festival

And the angel answered and said unto the women, Fear not ye: for I know that ye seek Jesus, which was crucified. He is not here; for he is risen, as he said. Come, see the place where the Lord lay. And go quickly, and tell his disciples that he is risen from the dead; and, behold, he goeth before you into Galilee; there shall ye see him. Matthew 28:5-7

Any Christian church that looks back to the crucifixion only with sorry tears, and is not pressing forward in the blessed life of the risen Christ, is no more than a "pitying kind of religion."

And I must agree with one of the old writers in the faith who said, "I cannot away with it!"—meaning, "I cannot tolerate this pitying kind of religion."

True spiritual power does not reside in the ancient

cross but rather in the victory of the mighty, resurrected Lord of glory who could pronounce after spoiling death: "All power is given unto me in heaven and in earth!" (Matt. 28:18)

Let us be confident, Christian brethren, that our power does not lie in the manger at Bethlehem nor in the relics of the cross.

The power of the believer lies in the triumph of eternal glory!

The Man who died on the cross died in weakness. The Bible is plain in telling us this. But He arose in power. If we forget or deny the truth and glory of His resurrection and the fact that He is seated at the right hand of God, we lose all the significance of the meaning of Christianity!

The resurrection of Jesus Christ brought about a startling change of direction. It is interesting and profitable to look at the direction of the prepositions in Matthew's account of the resurrection morning.

First, the women came *to* the tomb.

They came in love, but they came in sadness and fear, and they came to mourn. That was the direction of their religion before they knew Jesus had been raised from the dead. Their direction was towards the grave— the tomb which held the body of Jesus.

Many who still face in the direction of the tomb, knowing only mourning and grief, uncertainty and the fear of death, are all around us.

But on that historic resurrection day, the faithful women had a dramatic change of direction.

They heard the angelic news and they saw the evidence: "He is not here: for he is risen, as he said!" (Matt. 28:6) The mammoth stone had been rolled away and they themselves could see the stark emptiness of the tomb.

"Go quickly, and tell His disciples!"

So the record tells us they departed immediately *from* the sepulcher.

What an amazing change of direction! What a change wrought by the joyful news!

The preposition is now *from* the grave instead of *to* the grave. The direction is suddenly away from the tomb—because the tomb was empty and stripped of its age-old power.

The direction is suddenly no longer toward the end —for with Jesus alive from the dead and about to be glorified at the right hand of the Father, the direction changed toward endlessness—the eternity of eternal life and victory!

If this is not the message and meaning of Easter, the Christian church is involved in a shallow one-day festival each year, intent upon the brightness of colors and the fragrance of flowers and the sweet sentiments of poetry and spring time.

The Christian church should have its priorities in the right order.

Easter is not just a day in the church calendar, something to be celebrated each year as an end in itself, something that began early on that first day of the week and ended at midnight.

The resurrection morning was only the beginning of a great, grand and vast outreach that has never ended and will not end until our Lord Jesus Christ comes back again.

The reality of Easter and of the resurrection and of the great commission of the risen and ascending Christ is the reality of the great missionary priority of the Christian church throughout today's world.

The resurrection of Christ and the fact of the empty tomb are not a part of the world's complex and continuing mythologies. This is not a Santa Claus tale—it is history and it is reality.

The Christian church is helpless and hopeless if it is stripped of the reality and historicity of the bodily resurrection of Jesus Christ. The true church of Jesus Christ is necessarily founded upon the belief and the truth that it happened. There was a real death, there was a real tomb, there was a real stone. But, thank God, there was a sovereign Father in heaven, an angel sent to roll the stone away, and a living Saviour in a resurrected and glorified body able to proclaim to His disciples, "All power is given unto me in heaven and in earth!"

Since that is our prospect and hope, there is no reason for any of us to be continually asking for pity for the Lord Jesus Christ.

The church has too many radiant, beckoning opportunities to be occupied with this: "Let us kneel down by the cross and let us weep awhile."

It is wrong for us to join those whose concept seems to be that our Lord was a martyr, a victim of His own zeal, a poor pitiable Man with good intentions who found the world too big and life too much for Him. He is still portrayed by too many as sinking down in a helplessness wrought by death.

Why should we in His church walk around in black and continue to grieve at the tomb when the record clearly shows that He came back from death to prove His words: "All power is given unto me in heaven and in earth!"

Brethren, He died for us, but ever since the hour of resurrection, He has been the mighty Jesus, the mighty Christ, the mighty Lord!

Power does not lie with a babe in the manger.

Power does not lie with a man nailed and helpless on a cross.

Power lies with the man on that cross who gave His life, who went into the grave and who arose and came out on the third day, then to ascend to the right hand of the Father.

That is where power lies.

Our business is not to mourn and weep beside the grave.

Our business is to thank God with tearful reverence that He once was willing to go into that grave. Our business is to thank God for the understanding of what the cross meant and for understanding of what the resurrection meant both to God and to men.

Do we rightly understand the resurrection, in the sense that it placed a glorious crown upon all of Christ's sufferings?

Do we realize the full significance of our Lord Jesus Christ being seated today at the Father's right hand, seated in absolute majesty and kingly power, sovereign over every power in heaven and in earth?

There is always someone with a rejoinder: "But, Mr. Tozer, how can you back up that big talk? If Christ is sovereign over all the world, what about the world condition?

"What about Russia and spreading Communism?

"What about atom bombs and hydrogen bombs and impending doom?

"If He is sovereign, why is there a continuing armament race? Why does the Middle East situation continue to plague the entire world?"

There is an answer and it is the answer of the prophetic Scripture.

God has a prophetic plan in His dealing with the world, its nations and its governments.

God's plan will continue on God's schedule. His plan has always called for the return of Israel to Palestine. The nations of the earth are playing themselves into position all over the world—almost like a giant checker board—while God waits for the consummation.

While Israel gathers and while the King of the North beats himself out, the Christian church prays and labors to evangelize the world for the Saviour.

Christ waits—even though He has all the power. He waits to exercise His awesome power.

He is showing His power in many ways in the life and ministries of His church.

I believe He would exercise His unlimited power if His church would truly believe that He could and would do it!

When Jesus announced that "All power is given unto me in heaven and in earth," what did He expect His followers to do? What are the implications for all of us who are in the Body of Christ?

The answer is plain; Jesus said, "Go ye, therefore!"

Therefore is the word that connects everything together. Christ has been given all power; therefore we are to go and evangelize, discipling all nations. All of the implications of the resurrection add up to the fact that the Christian church must be a missionary church if it is to meet the expectations of the risen Saviour!

Because He is alive forevermore Jesus could promise, in the same context as His command, that He would be with us always, even unto the end of the world, or age.

There have been many little wall plaques and mottoes on display in Christian homes reading: "Lo, I am with you alway, even unto the end of the world." But that is only a partial quotation and it overrides certain implications.

You know how skillfully we take the knife of bad teaching and separate a little passage from the context even as we might take the rind from an orange. We peel the promise off and put it on our mottoes and calendars.

Let's be truthful and let our Lord say to us all exactly what He wants to say.

Is this what He said, "Lo, I am with you alway"?

Not exactly, my brother.

He actually said, "Go ye therefore, and teach all nations, baptizing them in the name of the Father, and of the Son, and of the Holy Ghost: teaching them to observe all things whatsoever I have commanded you: AND, LO, I AM WITH YOU ALWAY, EVEN UNTO THE END OF THE WORLD" (Matt. 28:19-20).

That little word *and* is not there by accident. Jesus literally was saying that His presence was promised and assured in the Christian church if the church continued faithful in its missionary responsibilities.

That's why I say that the resurrection of Jesus Christ is something more than making us the happiest fellows in the Easter parade.

Am I to listen to a cantata and join in singing "Up from the grave He arose," smell the flowers and go home and forget it?

No, certainly not!

It is truth and a promise with a specific moral ap-

103

plication. The resurrection certainty lays hold on us with all the authority of sovereign obligation.

It says that the Christian church is to go—to go into all the world, reaching and teaching all nations, or as the margin has it, "Make disciples among all nations."

So, the moral obligation of the resurrection of Christ is the missionary obligation, the responsibility and the privilege of carrying the message and telling the story, of praying and interceding, and of being involved personally and financially in the cause of this great commission.

I have asked myself many times why professing Christian believers can relegate the great missionary imperative of our Lord Jesus Christ to the sidelines of our Christian cause.

I cannot follow the reasoning of those who teach that the missionary commission given by Jesus Christ does not belong to the church but will be carried out during the great tribulation days emphasized in Bible prophecy.

I cannot give in to the devil's principal, deceitful tactic which makes so many Christians satisfied with an Easter celebration instead of experiencing the power of His resurrection. The enemy of our souls is quite happy about the situation when Christians make a big deal of Easter Sunday, put the emphasis on flowers and cantatas, and preachers use their soft-voiced and dewy-eyed technique in referring to Jesus as the greatest of all earth's heroes.

The devil is willing to settle for all of that kind of display as long as the churches stop short of telling the whole truth about the resurrection of Christ.

"It's fine with me if they just make a big hero of

Jesus, but I don't ever want them to remember for a minute that He is now seated in the place of power and I am actually a poor, frightened fugitive"—that's the reasoning of the devil.

And it is his business to keep Christians mourning awhile and weeping with pity beside the tree instead of demonstrating that Jesus Christ is risen indeed, is at the right hand of the Father in glory, and has the right and authority to put the devil in hell when the time comes, chaining him and hurling him down according to God's revealed prophetic plan.

The devil will do almost anything to keep us from actually believing and trusting that death has no more dominion and that Jesus Christ has been given all authority in heaven and in earth and hell, holding the keys thereof.

When will the Christian church rise up and get on the offensive for the risen and ascended Saviour?

When we come to know the full meaning of the cross and experience the meaning and the power of the resurrection in our own lives—that is the answer. Through the power of His resurrection we will take the spiritual offensive; we become the aggressors and our witness and testimony become the positive force in reaching the ends of the earth with the gospel.

We can just sum it all up by noting that Jesus Christ asks us only to surrender to His Lordship and obey His commands. He will supply the power if we will believe His promise and demonstrate the reality of His resurrection.

These promises of Christ have taken all the strain and pressure from our missionary responsibility. When the Spirit of God speaks and deals with our young people about their own missionary responsibility, Christ assures them of His presence and power as they prepare to go.

"All power is given unto Me. I am no longer in the grave. With all authority and power I can protect you, I can support you, I can go ahead of you, I can give you effectiveness in your witness and ministry. Go, therefore, and make disciples of all nations, and I will go with you. I will never leave you nor forsake you!"

Men without God suffer alone and die alone in time of war and in other circumstances of life. All alone!

But it can never be said that any true soldier of the cross of Jesus Christ, no man or woman as missionary or messenger of the truth has ever gone out to a ministry alone!

There have been many Christian martyrs—but not one of them was on that mission field all alone. No missionary that ever laid down his life in the jungle was actually alone—for Jesus Christ keeps His promise of taking him by the hand and leading him triumphantly through to the world beyond.

Do you see it, my friend? Resurrection is not a day of celebration—it is an obligation understood and accepted!

Because Jesus Christ is alive, there is something for us to do for Him every day. We cannot just sit down, settling back in religious apathy.

We can dare to fully trust the Risen One who said, "All power is given unto me in heaven and in earth . . . go ye therefore . . . and, lo, I am with you alway, even unto the end of the world."

Chapter Nine

Christian Uniformity:
An Evangelical Answer

Finally, be ye all of one mind, having compassion one of another, love as brethren . . . 1 Peter 3:8

Within the framework of evangelical Christianity, we do not pay a great deal of attention to current religious trends and fads. One of these in our day is the growing emphasis toward uniformity in the churches.

I think it is only fair, however, to reserve the right to put in our own word about the achievement of Christian unity, particularly in the face of continuing insistence that everyone in the church ought to be just like everyone else!

The Christian uniformity taught in the Bible can only come through genuine love and sincere compassion in the Christian fellowship. It can only come through the work of God in the soul of man—and then there can be unity even where there is a blessed and free diversity!

There is in Christian literature a statement by an old bishop that the uniformity we desire in the Christian church is not just a matter of achieving "solidarity"—for he reminds us that anyone can achieve a solid unity out of variety just by the freezing process!

We can distinguish this kind of frozen unity in the conduct of those churches where no one ever disagrees with anyone else because they all started out by agreeing that they would hold no basic tenet or positive belief "because nothing really matters that much anyhow."

But the apostle Peter writes to Christian brethren about the reality of "being of one mind" in their Christian fellowship.

Leading commentators tell us that the expression "being of one mind" literally means "unanimous."

So, let me tell you first what being unanimous is not, in order that we may discover what unanimity really is.

Being unanimous—spiritual unanimity—does not involve a regulated uniformity.

I cannot comprehend how the churches have fallen into the error of believing that unanimity means uniformity. Some actually hold that to be like-minded means the imposing of a similarity from the outside.

This has been a great error—the belief that harmony within religious bodies can be secured by imposing uniformity.

Look at the word *uniform*. In one use it is a word describing a situation, but it is also a noun referring to identifying garments worn by members of certain

108

groups. We have such uniforms in the armed services —various military uniforms.

Such garments provide a uniformity for military personnel—a uniformity imposed from the outside. But anyone who has ever served in the armed forces knows there is a world of disagreement and grousing among those who wear the uniforms.

Merely putting on the uniform does not in any sense bring about a basic unity and harmony in any group of men and women.

Imposed uniformity is a great error because it assumes that uniformity is an external thing and that it can be achieved by imposition, failing to acknowledge that the only valid unity is unity of the heart.

Actually, it is variety—and not uniformity—that is the hallmark of God. Wherever you see God's hand, you see variety rather than uniformity or similarity.

Paul tells us that one star differs from every other star in glory and when the "ceiling" lifts occasionally —ceiling being the word we use for all the smoke and grime and smog that lies over the city—we can all see the starry city of God and realize that no star is exactly like another. They differ from each other in glory for God made them.

If God had made all the stars in heaven according to a uniform pattern of size and distance from the earth, it would be like gazing at a glaring theater marquee rather than at the mysterious, wonderful heaven of God that we see when the skies are clear.

Anyone inclined to check can find out in five minutes that no two leaves on any tree are exactly alike. They all differ. They are somewhat alike—they may even be alike basically, but God allows them a certain freedom of variety in formation.

Visit the shore of any ocean and you will notice that even when the winds are high and the waves are running, there are no two waves exactly alike. If you look carelessly you may say they look alike, as there is a monotony and a uniformity as they roll in over the sand. But look more closely and you will agree that no two of them are alike.

The artist who paints the ocean waves all alike has imposed something of his own mind upon the Creator-God's work for the ocean is never guilty of repeating the same size and shape and formation even though the billows reach into numbers that man is unable to count.

As many of you know, the same rule is applied to birds. We may hear a bird song and say, "That bird is a cardinal—or a warbler," as the case may be.

We may say, "The one I hear singing is a robin."

But those who have been trained to listen and to listen closely tell us that no two robins sing exactly alike. It is a fact that is too well known to need any explanation.

Consider the Bible saints and the same rule. We make a great deal of similarities between Bible personalities when actually the variety is still more marked and apparent than the similarity.

Who can conceive of two men any more opposite than Isaiah and Elijah? If they had been sitting together in the same congregation, they would hardly have been recognized as belonging to the same race, let alone the same faith! Their similarities were within. They belonged together inside, but they certainly were different on the outside.

Or, take men like Peter and Moses and stand them up together. Or, just stay within the little circle of

Peter's own group, the disciples. Look at Philip, look at John, then on to the strong, Elijah-like Peter. Altogether unlike each other in variety of character and traits, yet their likeness was genuine and valid because it was a likeness within.

When God gave His church to the world, He gave a church that was to be unanimous within. But He also gave the church as much variety as an attractive flower garden.

I knew a dear man of God—a black man by the name of Collett—who used to preach. I have heard him say that "God makes His bouquets from the flowers which contain all His created colors. If they were all your color, there would be no variety, so God put me here in your midst to provide His variety."

He was perfectly right! God has His own variety throughout all the church, everywhere—not only in looks but in personality, in taste, in gifts and in ministries.

And yet Peter encourages us to be like-minded—to be unanimous!

What does he mean?

He means that the Spirit of God making Christ real within our beings will make us alike in certain qualities and disposition.

True Christian compassion is one of those qualities. Peter leaves us little doubt about the fruits of genuine Christian unanimity within. "Be alike compassionate. Be alike loving. Be alike pitiful. Be alike courteous . . . and be alike forgiving!"

Then he sums it all up: "Finally, be ye all of one mind."

This is the path to a blessed Christian unity and unanimity. This is the way to have one mind. Having compassion one for another, loving as brethren, having pity where it is needed, the willingness to be courteous, the ability that God gives to be forgiving in spirit, and not rendering evil for evil.

There you have the blessed uniformity of the children of God, the unanimity Peter was looking for among the followers of Christ. Every earnest believer must know the unanimity of compassion, the ability to love others, the uniformity of a spirit that can reach out in pity, the tenderness of heart that finds a true expression of God's grace in reaching out in a delightful courtesy and a willing forgiveness of others.

Are you willing to measure the compassion in your own spirit?

Compassion literally means a sympathetic understanding and wherever one life touches another there must be compassion if we are to please our Lord. This is what our true Christian unity demands—a likeness, a sympathetic understanding wherever our hearts touch, at every point of contact. We must be in agreement wherever our hearts touch.

This is the example we find in the Word of God— earnest men and women who touched God and where they touched Him they were alike. In other things they were different and not like each other at all. So it is to be in the Body of Jesus Christ, His church here on earth—that wherever we touch each other there is to be unity, but in all other things there can be diversity and variety. The variety among God's believing children is in itself an artistic scheme that God introduced to bring beauty to the church and its fellowship.

As an illustration, consider the variety of strings within a piano. They can all be combined to produce a beautiful oneness in harmony. All of the strings are different but they are alike in this—they all bow to a certain pitch. So, the believing people of God are alike in that they bow in recognition of the one holy, divine pitch to which they are to be set and keyed! After that, they can be just as unlike and as free to be themselves as they may be led.

I suppose there never was a body of Christians that succeeded in being freer than the Quakers even though they themselves did the best they could to choke it and kill it. They imposed a uniform and a certain dress, they imposed a certain use of language—but in spite of these they had so much of that inner flame that they succeeded in presenting to the world a wonderful flower-garden variety.

So, we must have the compassion of Christ within us, operating as a sympathetic understanding wherever we touch, with the agreement that it is possible for us to disagree in those areas where we do not touch.

Then Peter calls to mind the reality of loving one another. We are to love the brethren and love is oneness where hearts touch. This is a true and blessed unity—the feeling and the knowledge that the two have become one through the bonds of God's love. This is God's way, the genuine way, of bringing people together in a unity that is living and which will abide.

Now, without any desire to be on the side of disruptive elements in society, I must ask a question about the many insistent demands for getting everybody into some worldwide yoke of unity and uniformity:

"Why is it that the generation that is talking the most and making the most of unity is also the generation that has the greatest amount of hate and suspicion, the biggest bombs and the largest armies?"

They can't kid me! I refuse to be taken in by all of

the smooth talk and gentle assurances that "all men are brethren and we must all forget our differences because of the Fatherhood of God and the Brotherhood of Man."

They don't fool me because I know that there is no unity in the world—there is division and hatred and hostility and plenty of open strife which we don't call war if we can keep it localized. When they say, "Let's forget all the differences," I just want to have opportunity to feel and see if that lump is still on their hip—that lump that means a gun is still there!

God's love shed abroad in our hearts—compassion and love which can only be found in Jesus Christ, our Lord—these are the only elements of true unity among men and women today. All other emphasis on unity is a sadly strange and ironic joke that must have had its origin in the seventh hell below!

Is it possible to be a believing child of God and not be tender-hearted? Let me remind you that when Peter advises that Christian brethren are to be "full of pity" for one another, he is actually teaching us that our hearts are to be tender towards one another.

With this in mind, I must point out to you that religion will either make us very tender of heart, considerate and kind, or it will make us very hard.

Anyone who has studied history does not have to be informed that men and women can be very severe, engaging even in the worst of cruelties, explaining it all in the name of religion and "the principle" which is supposed to be involved.

I have a rule for myself here:

"Whose side am I on—principle or people?"

Within the history of our own American government, we bow in respect to one of our great presidents who was a man first and president second. They called him Honest Abe. He had a gift for sensing the humorous in life and a heart that cried easily over other people's sorrows.

During the Civil War, Lincoln had to deal with the military leaders who stood on ceremony and acted on principle in their treatment of young lads taken out of the hills and away from the farms, conscripted and sent with little training to the front lines of battle.

When the terror of gunfire and the screaming of the dying became overpowering, some of the boys turned away and fled in fear. When they were caught they were sentenced to die.

Along with his many other duties, Abraham Lincoln was busy doing everything he could to save these young men. One day his associates found him sadly turning over papers from a file and writing something at the bottom of each, one after another.

Someone asked, "What are you doing, Mr. President?"

"Tomorrow is 'butcher day' in the Army," he replied. "They are going to shoot my boys so I have been going over their papers once more to see if I can't get some of them off."

We love and honor the memory of Abe Lincoln for that kind of spirit. He was a man who loved people and was not ashamed of being tender in heart and full of pity for those in need. I do not mention Lincoln here to imply that he was a great Christian, for I am not a judge of that, but he was a great man and he had much that we Christians could borrow. I am convinced that he was a tender hearted, pitiful man who put people ahead of principle!

I don't have to tell you that principle has been a

hard, rough cross upon which human beings have been nailed throughout the centuries.

"There's a principle involved," zealous men have always cried as they nailed the man on the scaffold. His blood and tears and sweat never affected them at all because their pride assured them, "He is dying for a principle!"

Brethren, let people argue as they will; it is not principle that holds the moral world together, but rather the presence of a holy God and love for God and mankind!

Sure, moral laws exist in the world—and no one preaches that with any greater emphasis than I do. But to extract the principle from the holy and loving heart of God and then nail men on it is a far cry from the teaching and example of our Lord Jesus Christ.

Do you realize that Jesus never spent His time talking about principles? He always talked about people.

Even in His illustrative stories—the parables—He was not citing principles. He was talking about people —someone in trouble, someone gone astray or lost, someone sent out to bring other folks in. Always there were people.

Make of this what you will, but I don't think I would offer to give my life for a principle. I trust I would die for those I love. I trust that I would die for the church of Jesus Christ. I trust that I would give my everything for the love of God and the love of mankind. If I did not, I would surely be ashamed.

Now, that is one thing, but it is quite another thing to extract a stiff, iron principle and then nail a man on it, for God's Word tells us to be full of pity, tender of heart, loving and kind.

Jesus Christ did not come down from His place in

glory riding on a steel beam of divine principle—hard and stiff and cold.

Full of pity and love, tender hearted and submissive to the will of His Father on behalf of mankind, He went from the womb of the Virgin to the cross on Golgotha.

Of course He died for the moral government of Almighty God—but it was people He cared for and served. He achieved His end not by hardness and harshness and legal principle but by love and care and compassion for people. Back of it all, certainly, was the unchanging, divine principle—the moral righteousness of God, for the holiness of the deity must be sustained even if the world falls.

But being our divine Saviour and Lord, He walked in and out of His experiences with men and women with all sweetness and tenderness, never leaving an irritation or a scratch. We could well say that love lubricated His spirit as He loved the people—men and women and children, the low as well as the high.

There isn't anything that will make us more tender at heart and more compassionate in spirit than true religion—the true reception of the mercies of God. The Word of God plainly teaches that God our Father wants us to know the trusting spiritual life which makes us tender hearted and sensitive to His will. We see the contrast in the New Testament record of the proud and unbending religious life of the Pharisees—and how it gave them hardness of heart. Religion will do the one thing or the other!

Chapter Ten

The Presence of Christ: Meaning of the Communion

For I have received of the Lord that which also I deliv-
ered unto you, That the Lord Jesus the same night in
which he was betrayed took bread: And when he had
given thanks, he brake it, and said, Take, eat: this is
my body, which is broken for you: this do in remem-
brance of me. After the same manner also he took the
cup, when he had supped, saying, This cup is the new
testament in my blood: this do ye, as oft as ye drink
it, in remembrance of me. For as often as ye eat this
bread, and drink this cup, ye do shew the Lord's death
till he come. . . . He that eateth and drinketh unworth-
ily, eateth and drinketh damnation to himself, not dis-
cerning the Lord's body. 1 Corinthians 11:23-26, 29

It is amazing that many people seem to believe that
the Christian church is just another institution and

that the observance of communion is just one of its periodic rituals.

The Bible makes it plain that any church that is a genuine New Testament church is actually a communion and not an institution.

The dictionary says that a communion is a body of Christians having a common faith. Sharing and participation are other terms used in the definition of communion.

Regardless of traditions and terms and definition, the basic question in our coming to the Lord's table is this: "Have we come together to recognize the Presence of our divine Lord and risen Saviour?"

Brethren, how wonderful if we have found the spiritual maturity and understanding that allows us to confess: "Our congregation is so keenly aware of the presence of Jesus in our midst that our entire fellowship is an unceasing communion!"

What a joyful experience for us in this church age—to be part of a congregation drawn together with the magnetic fascination of the desire to know the presence of God and to sense His nearness.

The communion will not have ultimate meaning for us if we do not believe that our Lord Jesus Christ is literally present in the Body of Christ on earth.

There is a distinction here: Christ is literally present with us—but not physically present.

Some people approach the communion table with an awe that is almost fear because they think they are approaching the physical presence of God. It is a mistake to imagine that He is physically present.

Remember that God was not physically present in the burning bush of the Old Testament. Neither was He physically present between the wings of the cherubim in the tabernacle, nor in the cloud by day and fire by night.

In all these instances, He was literally present.

And so today, God who became Man—the Man who is God—this Man who is the focal point of divine manifestation, is here!

When we come to the Lord's table, we do not have to try to bring His presence. He is here!

He does ask, however, that we bring the kind of faith that will know and discern His presence; the kind of faith that will enable us to "forgive one another even as God for Christ's sake hath forgiven" us (Eph. 4:32).

Out of our worship and from the communion, God wants us to be able to sense the loving nearness of the Saviour—instantaneously bestowed!

There is nothing else like this in the world—the Spirit of God standing ready with a baptism of the sense of the presence of the God who made heaven and earth and holds the world in His hands. Knowing the sense of His presence will completely change our everyday life. It will elevate us, purify us, and deliver us from the domination of carnal flesh to the point where our lives will be a continuing, radiant fascination!

Here I want to refer back to Paul's message to the Corinthian church. We read and understand that there was trouble in that early church because the members came together for reasons other than recognizing the divine Presence.

Paul said they met without "discerning the Lord's body."

I have checked many sources of Christian scholarship, and I agree with Ellicott and other commentaries who believe this means that they met "without recognizing the Presence."

They were not required to believe that the bread and wine were God, but they were required to believe that God was present where Christians met to serve the bread and wine. Because they refused to recognize His presence, they were in great spiritual trouble.

Actually, they were meeting together for purposes other than that of finding God at the focal point of manifestation in the person of His Son!

There was a judgment upon them because they were too carnal, too worldly, too socially minded, too unspiritual to recognize that when Christians meet they should at least have the reverence that a Greek had when he led a heifer to the sacred grove. They should at least have the reverence that a Greek poet had when he quietly composed sonnets to his deity. When they came together they ought to have at least the reverence of a Jewish high priest of the Old Testament when he approached the sacred holy place and put blood upon the mercy seat.

But they came with another attitude. They did not come to commune in the Presence, and so the purpose and meaning of communion became vague.

It was true in other churches as well as set forth in Revelation 2 and 3.

Today, I say, we ought to be a company of believers drawn together to see and hear and feel God appearing in man. That man is not a preacher, or elder, or deacon, but the Son of Man, Jesus Christ—back from the dead and eternally alive!

It is impossible to separate the communion table from the centrality of Jesus Christ in the revealed Word of God.

Some think of communion as a celebration—and in the very best sense it is our Lord Jesus Christ whom we celebrate when we come to this table.

In order for us to grasp the spirit of this commemoration, notice the relationship of Christ, the Son of Man, in five words with their prepositions attached.

First, we celebrate Christ's "devotion to"—noting, for instance, His devotion to the Father's will.

Our Lord Jesus Christ had no secondary aims. His one passion in life was the fulfillment of His Father's will. Probably He was the only human being after the fall about whom this could be said in perfect terms. With any other person, it can be only an approximation. Realism requires that we say we suppose there never has been anyone who has not mourned the introduction, however brief, of some distraction.

But Jesus never had any distraction or deviation. His Father's will was always before Him, and it was to this one thing that He was devoted.

As part of that, He was devoted to the rescue of fallen mankind—completely devoted to it. He did not do a dozen other things as avocations. He did that one thing! He was devoted to the altar of sacrifice—to the rescue of mankind.

It may be helpful if I remind you about a famous symbol of one of the old Baptist missionary societies. It showed an ox quietly standing between an altar and a plow. Underneath was the legend, "Ready for either or for both!" Plow awhile, and then die on the altar. Or, only die on the altar or only plow awhile.

The meaning of the symbol was readiness—"ready for either or ready for both." I think it is one of the most perfect symbols that I have ever known picturing submission to God's will, and it certainly describes our Lord Jesus Christ.

He was ready first for His labors on earth, the work with the plow; to be followed by the altar of sacrifice. With no side interest, He moved with steady purpose—almost with precision—toward the cross. He would not be distracted nor turned aside. He was completely devoted to the cross, completely devoted to the rescue of mankind, because He was completely devoted to His Father's will!

Even "if we remain not faithful," as the Bible says, that does not change His faithful devotion. He has not changed. He is devoted as He was devoted! He came a devoted One, and the word *devoted* is actually a religious word referring to a sacrifice, usually a lamb that was selected and marked out. It was fed, it was cared for, but everyone considered it already dead on the altar of sacrifice.

It was the lamb that had been selected, and even though it waited in its place a few days, everyone knew of the coming sacrifice. They knew it was devoted. It was an expendable lamb. So, our Lord Jesus Christ was devoted—completely devoted as a lamb to the sacrifice!

Then, the second word is *separation* and the preposition is *from*. Devotion *to* and separation *from*.

There are many ways in which our Lord deliberately separated Himself. He separated Himself from men for men.

There are those who have separated themselves for other reasons. Tymen of Athens, you will remember, turned sour on the human race and went up into the hills, separating himself from mankind because he hated the human race. His separation was the result of hatred. But the separation of Jesus Christ from men was the result of love. He separated Himself from them for them. It was for them He came—and died. It was for them that He arose and ascended and for them appeared at the right hand of God.

This separation from men was not because He was weary of them, nor that He disliked them. Rather, it was because He loved them. It was a separation in order that He might do for them that which they could not do for themselves. He was the only one who could rescue them. So Jesus was a separated man from the affairs of man.

Separation from is the phrase that marks Him. He was separated from the net of trivialities. There are so many things that are done in the world by Christians that are not really bad—they are just trivial. They are unworthy, much as if we found Albert Einstein busy cutting out paper dolls. Though deeply disappointed, no one would go to him and say, "Einstein, that's a great sin you are committing." But we would go away shaking our heads and saying, "With a mind like that? One of the six great minds of the ages— cutting paper dolls!"

There are so many trivialities in which great minds seem to engage. Yes, your mind, I mean! Great minds.

You smile and say, "Me?"

Yes, I do mean you!

I mean your mind with its endless capabilities. I mean your spirit with its potential for angelic fellowship and divine communion. Yet we engage in trivialities.

Jesus was never so engaged—He escaped the net of trivialities!

He was separated from sinners, it says in the Bible. He was separated not only from their sins, but separated from their vanities. Vanities. Separated from!

Do I need to remind you in this context that if these words characterized Jesus, they must also characterize each of us who claims to be a follower of Jesus?

Devotion to! Yes, devotion to the Father's will; devotion to the rescue of mankind by the preaching of the gospel; devotion to any necessary sacrifice, having no interests aside, but moving with steady purpose to do the will of God!

Separation from! But not in sourness nor contempt, but like the runner, separated from his regular clothing in order that he might strip himself for the race—or like a soldier separated from his civilian garb in order to wear only that which is prescribed to free his arms and legs for combat. It is this separation we must know as His loving disciples.

The third word is *rejection* and this is the phrase of *rejection by*.

Plainly, Jesus suffered rejection by mankind because of His holiness. Then He suffered rejection by God because of His sinfulness. But someone will say, "Wait a minute! Would you say our Lord was sinful?"

Yes, vicariously sinful.

He Himself never sinned, but He that knew no sin became sin for us, that we sinners might become the righteousness of God in Him.

In that sense, He suffered a twofold rejection. He was too good to be received by sinful men and in that awful moment of His sacrifice He was too sinful to be received by a holy God. So He hung between heaven and earth rejected by both until He cried, "It is finished. Father, into Thy hand I commend my spirit." Then He was received by the Father.

But while He was bearing my sins and yours, He

was rejected by the Father. While He moved among men He was rejected by them because He was so holy that His life was a constant rebuke to them.

Identification with should also be noted. Surely He was identified with us. Everything He did was for us. He acted in our stead. He took our guilt. He gave us His righteousness. In all of these acts on earth, it was for us because by His incarnation, He identified Himself with the human race. In His death and resurrection He was identified with the redeemed human race.

The blessed result is that whatever He is we are; and where He is, potentially, His people are, and what He is, potentially, His people are—only His deity being excepted!

Finally, consider His *acceptance at.*

Jesus Christ, our Lord, has acceptance at the throne of God. Although once rejected, He is now accepted at—and that bitter rejection is now turning into joyous acceptance. The same is true for His people. Through Him, we died! Identified with Him, we live, and in our identification with Him we are accepted at the right hand of God, the Father.

This is the meaning of our celebration. Surely I do not need a picture of the holy family to remind me. Surely I do not need to wear beads around my neck to remind me.

If my love for Him does not remind me 24 hours a day, then I simply need to confess and repent and ask for the restoring of the grace and mercy of God that will keep me always in remembrance!

One of the great Scottish dissenters who lived in the last century was Horatius Bonar. He belonged to the Free Church of Scotland which came into being through a break with the state church. A critic of his once said:

"Bonar was a wonderfully good man and a wonderfully gifted man, but his imagination led him astray. His imagination led him to believe that Jesus Christ was coming back to raise the dead and change the living, and that He was going to restore Israel to the Holy Land, and transform the church and bless mankind, destroy the anti-Christ with the brightness of His coming."

The critic went on to say it was too bad that Bonar went so far astray.

In reply, we say that if he went so far "astray" as to believe that, perhaps that is why he could write hymns that said, "I heard the voice of Jesus say, Come unto me and rest" and "I lay my sins on Jesus, the spotless Lamb of God."

He wrote this about the Lord's Supper:

Here, O my Lord, I see Thee face to face;
Here would I touch and handle things unseen,
Here grasp with firmer hand th'eternal grace,
And all my weariness upon Thee lean.

Here would I feed upon the bread of God,
Here drink with Thee the royal wine of heaven;
Here would I lay aside each earthly load,
Here taste afresh the calm of sins forgiven.

This is the hour of banquet and of song;
This is the heavenly table spread for me;
Here let me feast, and feasting, still prolong
The brief bright hour of fellowship with Thee.

Too soon we rise; the symbols disappear;
The feast, though not the love, is past and gone;

The bread and wine removed, but Thou art here,
*   Nearer than ever; still my Shield and Sun.*

Mine is the sin, but Thine the righteousness;
*   Mine is the guilt, but Thine the cleansing blood;*
Here is my robe, my refuge, and my peace,
*   Thy blood, Thy righteousness, O Lord my God.*

Feast after feast thus comes and passes by,
*   Yet passing, points to the glad feast above,*
Giving sweet foretaste of the festal joy,
*   The Lamb's great bridal feast of bliss and love.*

So, my brethren, the Lord's table, the communion, is not as a picture hung on the wall or a chain around the neck reminding us of Him.

It is a celebration of His person—a celebration in which we gladly join because we remember Him, testifying to each other and to the world of His conquering and sacrificial death—until He comes!

Chapter Eleven

Don't Ever Lose Hope:
You Can Be Changed

As obedient children, not fashioning yourselves accord-
ing to the former lusts in your ignorance: but as he
which hath called you is holy, so be ye holy in all
manner of conversation. 1 Peter 1:14-15

The Christian church cannot effectively be Christ's
church if it fails to firmly believe and boldly proclaim
to every person in the human race: "You can be
changed! You do not have to remain as you are!"

Brethren, this is not just a hope held out to the
desperate dope addict and the helpless drunkard—it is
the hope of every average sinner no matter where he
may be found in the world.

Shall we heed what the Holy Spirit is trying to say
to us about human nature and God's grace in this
apostolic injunction?

"Not fashioning yourselves according to the former lusts"—here is a truth negatively stated but carrying with it a positive assertion. We all know from our studies how every concept carries its opposite along with it in its understanding.

For instance, if you say "short," the opposite, "long," is conjured up in the back of your mind. Otherwise, there would be no reason to call something short.

Notice that the Apostle did not say, "Do not fashion yourselves . . ."—that would be contrary to Scripture and contrary to human nature.

His injunction is: Fashion not yourself after the old pattern, the pattern of your former lusts in your ignorance.

So, it is the positive element that we consider. Certainly and positively you will fashion yourselves, but do not fashion yourselves after the old pattern, we are cautioned.

This is at the insistence of the Holy Spirit, and the Scriptures give no room for argument here. We are given no excuse whatsoever to read this, or sit in a church service and find fault with what the Holy Spirit says. You may have reason to disagree with an interpretation given by the preacher, but that is another matter. Once we know what the Holy Spirit has said, as believers we are committed to carry out that injunction without one word of objection. What else should we do with the Word of God but obey?

So, our English word, *fashion*, expresses the Apostle's admonition that Christian believers ought to shape themselves according to proper pattern.

"Fashion yourselves—conform yourselves to the right pattern" is what Peter was actually saying.

In essence, Peter was also stressing a most important fact, that human nature is fluid. Human nature is not fixed and unchangeable as many people seem to believe.

Perhaps clay is the very best illustration to give us a simple understanding of this biblical principle.

Clay is not fixed. It is malleable. In a figurative sense it is "fluid" so it can be shaped.

After clay has been fashioned and shaped by the potter, after he has given it the form that he wants, he puts it into the oven. He bakes it and burns it and then, perhaps, he glazes it.

That clay is now permanently fixed. It is no longer fluid, no longer subject to any changes. The only way it can be changed now is by being destroyed. It can be crushed and ruined, but it can never be changed into something more beautiful and useful because it can never regain its fluid and malleable state.

I believe, then, that the very fact that the Holy Spirit would indicate through the Apostle, "Fashion and shape yourselves after the right pattern," makes it plain that the burning and baking and glazing have not yet happened to human nature. Thankfully we are in a state of fluidity regarding moral character.

Now, there are two things that can be said about any person, whether it is a youngster or the man sitting in the death cell of the state prison awaiting his fate for kidnapping and murder.

The first thing that can be said is: "You can be changed!" The second thing is like unto it: "You are not finished yet!"

We hear a lot about men being hardened, but we should always remember that we need modifiers if we are going to get at the truth.

When we say that a man is hardened and that he

133

is beyond help, we are saying that insofar as any power and influence that we may have, the man is probably in a state beyond our changing.

But actually and in truth, no one is beyond changing as long as he is alive and conscious!

The hope may be dim in many cases, but the hope of change does exist for every man. It may be a dim hope for the drunkard who allows himself only a few sober moments for serious thought, but he may be saved from complete despair by the knowledge that he can be changed.

It is still a hope even for the drug addict who is in frightful misery and who would sell his own soul to get the shot for the fix to carry him through one more day. The only reason he does not commit suicide is that faint flicker of hope that he can still be changed. He knows that he has not yet been cast or glazed in a final, unchangeable state—there is still a fluidity.

Let us thank God that there is that kind of hope, and the possibility of great change even for those who would likely be written off by our own human judgment. History has truly and completely confirmed this possibility.

The blessed aspect of this truth is that there is no sinner anywhere in the world who is compelled to remain as he is today.

He may be floundering in his sin, so deeply enmeshed that he is ashamed of himself. But the very fact that he is ashamed indicates that there is a model and a pattern to which he may still attain. It is this hope of change that keeps men alive on the earth.

The second part of this ray of hope for any man is the prospect that he is not yet "finished."

I dare to say that whoever you are and wherever

you may be, old or young or in-between, you are not yet a finished product. You are only in process.

I admit that it is our human tendency to fix certain terminal points and to say, "Beyond these we do not go."

Take human birth for instance.

Looking at birth in one way, we recognize that the obstetrician, after examining the new baby and finding it healthy, may say: "Now this is fixed. As far as I am concerned, a child is born into the world, and my part is complete." He fixes a terminal point there and goes about his other concerns.

During the months just preceding he was very anxious and concerned. For him, the terminal point has now been reached—a healthy, normal child has been born into the world.

But the mother of the child does not join in any terminal point at this juncture. She knows there is a tiny life involved and she knows the long continuing process which lies ahead. She knows of the childhood problems and troubles. She knows the educational process ahead from the time she teaches him to play patty-cake until he walks out of the college hall with his degree. The child is not "fixed"—there is the long process of shaping and fashioning.

Then when he has gotten his college degree, the parents are likely to rejoice and fix their own terminal point: "Well, we have succeeded in getting him through college!" Parents have a tendency to put a period there and say, "Now he is finished. He is complete."

But beyond all of that we know the truth—he is not done. He is not finished. There are still many changes to come and he is still being shaped and fashioned.

There will soon be another terminal point—his marriage. Many a mother breathes a sigh of relief when the child suddenly becomes serious, settles down, gets married, establishes a home.

Her sigh is really her way of saying within: "Now my worries are over!"

But not everything and everyone that is settled down is finished either. Parents are gratified when success comes and their boy becomes vice president of his company, drawing a big check and driving an expensive car.

The parents smile at each other and say, "Now he is fixed. He has arrived. He is a big American businessman!" It is not easy for parents to look beyond this pleasant terminal point.

But their child is still moving along. He will come to middle age when, as the poet said, "Gray hairs are here and there upon him." The parents comment that his gray hairs really give him a distinguished look and they cannot conceive that things will ever really change for him.

"He has really arrived," is their consolation. "He is a portly, well-proportioned businessman, an executive. He hunts in the fall and fishes in the spring and goes to baseball games in the summer—all the things that professional businessmen do. Don't worry about him. He is fixed!"

But he is a human being, and he is not fixed. He will never be finished until the soul leaves the body. Even the old man in his dotage is still changing in some ways. The rapidity and scope of change may not be as great, but there is change nevertheless.

It is at this point that someone will want to establish a dialogue. Someone will say, "Oh, yes, Mr. Tozer, but I do know a terminal point. You have been talking in terms of humanity, unregenerate humanity. The fixed point, the terminal point is the time of our conversion to Christ."

Yes, there is a point there when we can say, "Now rest my long-divided heart, fixed on this blissful center, rest!"

But does our conversion to Christ and our assurance of forgiveness mean that the fluidity in our nature is gone and that we are finally "fixed"?

My friend, the answer is "No!" You are still fluid. You are still subject to being fashioned and changed and shaped. God expects that you will still grow and develop and change and be fashioned as a Christian in maturity and Christlikeness.

Peter was recognizing that Christian believers are still in process when he wrote, "Do not fashion yourselves after the old pattern but after a new and holy pattern!"

I think there are many followers of Christ who have never been brought into this realization and understanding. Perhaps Christian workers are at fault at this point, when we work so hard to get people converted and then put a period after their conversion and speak the comfortable words: "Now rest your long-divided heart!"

There is a sense in which that old hymn is beautifully, brilliantly true and I love it and sing it often. But I am sure that the writer was not intending to imply a terminal point. I am sure he was not suggesting that the believer is no longer fluid, malleable. The fact is that he was assuring us that our being fixed in Christ is settled by an act of faith—and that's what we mean. But when it comes to the shaping and developing and growth and enlargement—these must go on after we are converted!

I expect some objections here from the people who would insist that Christians cannot fashion themselves.

"God must fashion us. God is our heavenly Father and He must do the fashioning and changing," they point out.

Let me agree this far: that is the ideal and that is the way it *should* be.

If every believer could be completely and wholly surrendered from the moment he is saved until the time he dies, knowing nothing but the influences of God and the heavenly powers working in him, then that would be true.

But there are powers that shape men even in the kingdom of God, that are not divine powers.

Let me use an illustration here of the person interested in getting a sun tan, exposing himself to the sun at the beach or in his own back yard.

Now, who is tanning his hide? Where is the tan coming from? What does the person himself have to do with it?

There is a sense in which he is doing it, for if he had kept his shirt on, his shoulders and body would never be tanned.

But there is a sense in which the sun is doing it. The sun is tanning him, but he had to take the necessary step to cooperate with the rays of the sun in order for the sunlight to do its work.

Now, that is exactly what we mean when we say that we fashion ourselves. A Christian believer fashions himself by exposing himself to the divine powers which shape him. Just as a man may wear his jacket and never get the sun tan, even though the sun is up there brightly in view, so a Christian may keep himself wrapped in a cloak of his own stubbornness and never receive any of the beneficial graces which filter down from the throne of God where Jesus sits as mediator.

Yes, it is possible for a Christian to go through life without very much change taking place. Converted? Yes. A believer in Christ? Yes. Having the root of the matter in him? Yes. The seed of God in him? Yes.

But such a believer is infantile and the growth and development and beautifying and enlarging and shaping have not taken place because he refuses to cooperate and expose himself to the divine powers that would shape him.

The reverse side of this proposition must also be considered. It is entirely possible for the Christian believer to shape himself by exposing himself to the wrong kind of influences. I think this is happening to an extent that must indeed be a grievance to God.

Now, what about these powers that can fashion us?

We know full well what the old powers were. Those old powers were the "former lusts."

The Apostle soberly reminds us of those powers in the second chapter of Ephesians:

"Wherein in time past ye walked according to the course of this world, according to the prince of the power of the air, the spirit that now worketh in the children of disobedience; among whom also we all had our conversation in times past in the lusts of our flesh, fulfilling the desires of the flesh and of the mind; and were by nature the children of wrath, even as others" (2:2-3).

Those were the forces which had a part in shaping us in our past. But now, even though weary, worn and sad, we have come to the Saviour and found in Him a resting place. And He has made us glad!

Therefore, we are encouraged to put away those old forces. We are not to expose ourselves to them any more.

But the question is often raised: "How can I hold myself from being shaped? I am thrown daily among the people of this world. I work in a situation where men are wicked and vulgar and obscene."

Here's my answer: You must engage your own will in the direction of God's will for your life. You can keep yourself from being shaped by your situation just as a man on the beach can keep himself from being tanned by the sun. You can draw your being tightly up in faith by an act of your will and take a positive stand: "Stay out, you devilish influences, in the name of my Saviour! Let my soul alone—it belongs to God!"

Many of our students can tell of the dirty talk and irreverence in their schools. Some of our Christian young people have even found a way to turn those things to personal spiritual blessing. Hearing an obscenity, they have an instant reaction and a compensation within: "Oh, God, I hate that so much that I want you to make my own mind and speech cleaner than it ever was before!"

Seeing an injurious, wicked habit in others, they look within at once and breathe a silent prayer: "Oh, God, you are able to keep me and shield me from this thing!"

It is possible, even in this sensuous world with its emphasis on violence and filth, that we can use those very things and react or compensate in the direction of God's promised victory. We are assured in the Word of God that we do not have to yield in weakness to the pull that would drag us down.

When we see something that we know is wrong and displeasing to Him, we can react to it with a positive assurance as we say: "God helping me, I will be different from that!" In that sense, the very sight of evil can drive us farther into the kingdom of God.

Now, what can we put into practice from this approach?

I share with you a few very simple thoughts about basic things in our own day that have powers to shape us, whether or not we are Christians. These are everyday things, and they have influence upon our lives, whether we know it or not, whether we believe it or not, or whether we like it or not.

What can you say about the kinds of books and magazines you read? The things you read will fashion you by slowly conditioning your mind. Little by little, even though you think you are resisting, you will take on the shape of the mind of the author of that book you are reading. You will begin to put your emphasis where he puts his. You will begin to put your values where he places his. You will find yourself liking what he likes and thinking as he thinks.

The same thing is certainly true of the power of modern films on the minds and morals of those who give themselves over to their influences.

Then, what about the kind of music you enjoy?

It seems almost too late in these times to try to give a warning that many in our society seem to revel in—the vile and vicious and obscene words of gutter songs. But there are other accepted types of music just as dangerous and just as damaging to the human spirit, just as harmful to the soul.

141

It is not overstating the case to insist that the kinds of music you enjoy will demonstrate pretty much what you are like inside.

If you give yourself to the contemporary fare of music that touches the baser emotions, it will shape your mind and emotions and desires, whether you admit it or not.

You can drink poison if you want to, but I am still friend enough to warn you that if you do, you will be carried out in a box. I cannot stop you but I can warn you. Nor do I have authority to tell you what you should listen to, but I have a divine commission to tell you that if you love and listen to the wrong kinds of music your inner life will wither and die.

Think with me also about the kind of pleasures in which you indulge.

If we should start to catalog some of your pastimes, you would probably break in and ask: "What's wrong with this?" and "What's wrong with that?"

There probably is no answer that will completely satisfy you if you are asking the question, but this is the best answer: "Give a person ten years in the wrong kind of indulgence and questionable atmosphere and see what happens to the inward spiritual life."

The pleasures in which we indulge selfishly will shape us and fashion us over the years, for whatever gives us pleasure has the subtle power to change us and enslave us.

What are the fond ambitions you entertain for your life?

The dream of whatever you would like to be will surely influence and shape you. It will also lead to choices of the places where you spend your time. I realize that we are not going to be very successful in advising people where they should go and should not go. Just the same, those who are on their way to heaven through faith in God's Son and God's plan should be careful of the kind of places they frequent, because these will shape and leave their imprint on man's spirit and soul.

We would do well to consider also the kind of words we speak.

Of all the people in the world I have read about, I think American people must be the most careless with language and expression.

For instance, any typical American joke must be an exaggeration. Mark Twain used the device of exaggeration, and it has become an accepted form not only of comedy but of communication among Americans. Are you watching your own language and are you careful of your own expressions in view of what it could mean to the effectiveness of your own Christian testimony?

Next, consider how important it is to make and cherish the right kind of friends in this life.

I value friendship very highly. I know we can appreciate and honor one another in friendship, even in this wicked world.

Because it is possible that friendships can be beautiful and helpful, I have always felt something like a churlish heel to stand before an audience and insist: "You must break off certain friendships if you want to truly serve God."

But our Lord Jesus said it more plainly and more bluntly than I could ever say it. He told us that in being His disciples we must take up our cross and follow Him and there would be instances when we must turn our backs on those who would hold us back—

even our own relatives and close friends. Jesus Christ must be first in our hearts and minds and it is He who reminds us that the salvation of our souls is of prime importance.

Better to have no friends and be an Elijah, alone, than to be like Lot in Sodom, surrounded by friends who all but damned him. If you give your cherished friendship to the ungodly counsellor and the scorner, you have given the enemy the key to your heart. You have opened the gate and the city of your soul will be overwhelmed and taken!

Finally, what kind of thoughts do we spend our time brooding over?

It is quite evident that for every murder or robbery, an embezzlement or other evil deeds, someone has spent long hours brooding over the idea, the plans, the chance of gain or the hope of revenge. In our great increasing wave of crime and violence, every deed is conditioned or preceded by some brooding thoughts.

Whatever thoughts you are willing to brood over in the night seasons will shape you and form you. The thoughts you entertain can change you from what you are into something else, and it will not be for the better unless your thoughts are good thoughts.

In the light of all these influences, Paul appeals to us all: "Be not conformed . . . but be transformed!" You do have a soul and you have influences that will shape you. God gives the clay to the potter and says, "Now, shape it!" God gives the material to the builder and says, "Now, build it into a worthy temple!"

Then, God says at last, "How did you shape it? How did you fashion it? What do you have to bring me from the material that I gave you? What did you do with those forces and influences that came to you daily?"

I trust that in that last great day none of us will have to stand before the judgment seat of Christ and confess with shame that we allowed unworthy things to have a place in shaping our lives.

Rather, it is time now to be transformed by the renewing of our minds that we may know what is the perfect and acceptable will of God!

Chapter Twelve

The Second Coming:
Doctrine on the Blessed Hope

And when he had spoken these things, while they beheld, he was taken up; and a cloud received him out of their sight. And while they looked stedfastly toward heaven as he went up, behold, two men stood by them in white apparel; which also said, Ye men of Galilee, why stand ye gazing up into heaven? this same Jesus, which is taken up from you into heaven, shall so come in like manner as ye have seen him go into heaven. Acts 1:9-11

Only the Christian church in the midst of all the world religions is able to proclaim the Bible's good news that God, the Creator and Redeemer, will bring a new order into being!

Indeed, it is the only good news available to a fallen race today—the news that God has promised a new order that is to be of eternal duration and infused with eternal life.

How amazing!

It is a promise from God of a new order to be based upon the qualities which are the exact opposite of man's universal blight—temporality and mortality!

God promises the qualities of perfection and eternity which cannot now be found in mankind anywhere on this earth.

What a prospect!

We are instructed that this new order, at God's bidding, will finally show itself in the new heaven and the new earth. It will show itself in the city that is to come down as a bride adorned for her husband.

The Word of God tells us that all of this provision for the redeemed has the quality of eternal duration.

It is not going to come just to go again. It is not to be temporal.

It is a new order that will come to stay.

It is not going to come subject to death. It is not to be mortal.

It is a new order that will come to live and remain forever!

God in His revelation to man makes it very plain that the risen Christ Jesus is the Head of this new creation and that His church is the Body. It is a simple picture, instructing us that individual believers in the risen Christ are the Body's members.

It seems to me that this is revealed so clearly in the Bible that anyone can see it and comprehend it.

The whole picture is there for us to consider.

The first Adam—the old Adam—was the head of everything in that old order, so when he fell, he pulled everything down with him.

I know that there are some bright human beings who argue against the historicity of the fall of human kind in Adam and Eve. But no man, however brilliant, wise, and well-schooled, has been able to escape two brief sentences written across all of his prospects by the great God Almighty.

Those sentences are: "Man, you cannot stay—you must go!" and "Man, you cannot live—you must die!"

No human being, regardless of talents and possessions and status, has yet won a final victory over his sentence of temporality and mortality.

Temporality says, "You must go!"

Mortality says, "You must die!"

Because this is true, then all of the works that men do actually partake of what man is. The same blight that rests upon sinful, fallen man—namely, temporality and mortality—rests upon every work that man does.

Mankind has many areas of life and culture of which he is proud. Man has long used such words as beauty, nobility, creativity and genius. But all the work of a man's hand, however noble it may be, however inspired by genius, however beautiful and useful—still has these two sentences written across it: "You cannot stay!" and "You cannot live!"

It is still only the work and hope and dream of fallen man and God continually reminds him, "You came only to go and you came surely to die!"

Everything and anything, whether a sonnet or an oratorio, a modern bridge or a great canal, a famous painting or the world's greatest novel—every one has God's mark of judgment upon it. Temporality and mortality!

Not one can remain—it is in the process of going.

149

Not one is eternal—it is only the work of fallen man who must die. And all of the work that man does cannot escape the sentence of partaking of what man is.

But a second man, the new and last Adam, came into this world to bring the promise of a new and eternal order for God's creation. The Son of Man, Christ Jesus the Lord, came and died, but rising from the grave, lives forever that He might be the Head of the new creation.

God's revelation says that Jesus Christ is the eternal Victor, triumphant over sin and death! That is why He is the Head of the new creation which has upon it the banner of perfectivity rather than temporality and the mark of life forevermore rather than the mark of death.

When we think of the ebb and flow of man's history and the inability of men to thwart the reality of death and judgment, it seems incredible that proud men and women—both in the church and outside the church—refuse to give heed to the victorious eternal plan and program of Jesus Christ!

Most of the reasons for the neglect of Christ's promises are all too evident among us today.

For one thing, modern man is too impatient to wait for the promises of God. He takes the short-range view of things.

He is surrounded by gadgets that get things done in a hurry. He has been brought up on quick oats; he likes instant coffee, he wears drip-dry shirts and takes 30-second Polaroid snapshots of his children.

His wife shops for her spring hat before the leaves fall to the ground in autumn. His new car, if he buys it after July 1, is already an old model when he brings it home.

He is almost always in a hurry and can't bear to wait for anything.

This breathless way of living naturally makes for a mentality impatient of delay, so when this man enters the kingdom of God he brings his short-range psychology with him. He finds prophecy too slow for him. His first radiant expectations soon lose their luster.

He is likely, then, to inquire: "Lord, wilt thou at this time restore again the kingdom to Israel?"

When there is no immediate response, he may conclude, "My Lord delayeth his coming!"

Actually, it has taken some people a long time to discover that the faith of Christ offers no buttons to push for quick service. The new order must wait for the Lord's own time—and that is too much for the man in a hurry.

He just decides to give up and becomes interested in something else.

Also, there is little question that the prevailing affluence of our society has much to do with the general disregard of Christ's promises that He would come to earth again to intervene in human history.

If the rich man enters the kingdom of God with difficulty, then it is logical to conclude that a society having the highest percentage of well-to-do persons in it will have the lowest percentage of Christians, all things else being equal.

If the "deceitfulness of riches" chokes the Word and makes it unfruitful, then this would be the day of near-fruitless preaching, at least in the opulent West.

And if surfeiting and drunkenness and worldly cares tend to unfit the Christian for the coming of

Christ, then this generation of Christians should be the least prepared for that event.

On the North American continent, Christianity has become the religion of the prosperous middle and upper middle classes almost entirely; the very rich or the very poor rarely become practicing Christians.

The touching picture of the poorly dressed, hungry saint, clutching his Bible under his arm and with the light of God shining in his face, hobbling painfully toward the church, is chiefly imaginary.

One of the most irritating problems of even an ardent Christian these days is to find a parking place for the shiny chariot that transports him effortlessly to the house of God where he hopes to prepare his soul for the world to come.

In the United States and Canada the middle class today possesses more earthly goods and lives in greater luxury than emperors and Maharajas did only a century ago.

There surely can be little argument with the assumption that since the bulk of Christians comes from this class, it is not difficult to see why the genuine expectation of Christ's return has all but disappeared from among us.

It is hard indeed to focus attention upon a better world to come when a more comfortable one than this can hardly be imagined. As long as science can make us so cozy in this present world it is admittedly hard to work up much pleasurable anticipation of a new world order even if it is God who has promised it.

Beyond these conditions in society, however, is the theological problem—too many persons holding an inadequate view of Jesus Christ Himself.

Ours is the age in which Christ has been explained,

humanized, demoted. Many professing Christians no longer expect Him to usher in a new order. They are not at all sure that He is able to do so; or if He does, it will be with the help of art, education, science and technology—that is, with the help of man.

This revised expectation amounts to disillusionment for many. And, of course, no one can become too radiantly happy over a King of kings who has been stripped of His crown or a Lord of lords who has lost His sovereignty.

Another facet of the problem is the continuing confusion among teachers of prophecy, some of whom seem to profess to know more than the prophets they claim to teach.

This may be in the realm of history, but it was only a little more than a short generation ago, around the time of the first World War, that there was a feeling among gospel Christians that the end of the age was near and there was anticipation and hope of a new world order about to emerge.

In the general outline of the scriptural hope, this new order was to be preceded by a silent return of Christ to earth, not to remain, but to raise the righteous dead to immortality and to glorify the living saints in the twinkling of an eye. These He would catch away to the marriage supper of the Lamb, while the earth meanwhile plunged into its baptism of fire and blood in the Great Tribulation. This would be relatively brief, ending dramatically with the battle of Armageddon and the triumphant return of Christ with His Bride to reign a thousand years.

Let me assure you that those expectant Christians had something very wonderful which is largely lacking today. They had a unifying hope. Their activities were concentrated. They fully expected to win.

Today, our Christian hope has been subjected to so much examination, analysis and revision that we are embarrassed to admit that we believe there is genuine substance to the hope we espouse.

Today, professing Christians are on the defensive, trying to prove things that a previous generation never doubted. We have allowed unbelievers to get us in a corner and have given them the advantage by permitting them to choose the time and place of encounter.

We smart under the attack of the quasi-Christian unbeliever, and the nervous, self-conscious defense we make is called "the religious dialogue."

Under the scornful attack of the religious critic, real Christians, who ought to know better, are now "rethinking" their faith.

Worst of all, adoration has given way to celebration in the holy place, if indeed any holy place remains to this generation of confused Christians.

In summary, I think that we must note that there is a vast difference between the doctrine of Christ's coming and the hope of His coming.

It surely is possible to hold the doctrine without feeling a trace of the blessed hope. Indeed there are multitudes of Christians today who hold the doctrine—but what I have tried to deal with here is that overwhelming sense of anticipation that lifts the life upward to a new plane and fills the heart with rapturous optimism. It is my opinion that this is largely lacking among us now.

Frankly, I do not know whether or not it is possible to recapture the spirit of anticipation that animated the early Christian church and cheered the hearts of gospel Christians only a few decades ago.

Certainly scolding will not bring it back, nor arguing over minor points of prophecy, nor condemning those who do not agree with us. We may do all or any of these things without arousing the desired spirit of joyous expectation. That unifying, healing, purifying hope is for the childlike, the innocent-hearted, the unsophisticated.

Brethren, let me tell you finally that all those expectant believers in the past have not been wholly wrong. They were only wrong about the time. They saw Christ's triumph as being nearer than it was, and for that reason their timing was off; but their hope itself was valid.

Many of us have had the experience of misjudging the distance of a mountain toward which we were traveling. The huge bulk that loomed against the sky seemed very near, and it was hard to persuade ourselves that it was not receding as we approached.

So the City of God appears so large to the minds of the world-weary pilgrim that he is sometimes the innocent victim of an optical illusion; and he may be more than a little disappointed when the glory seems to move farther away as he approaches.

But the mountain is really there—the traveler need only press on to reach it. And the Christian's hope is substance, too; his judgment is not always too sharp, but he is not mistaken in the long view—he will see the glory in God's own time!